INTRODUCTION

To his Greek and Roman adversaries the Celtic warrior was the archetypal barbarian: huge in stature, immensely strong and bloodthirsty beyond description. Charging naked into battle, impervious to wounds and wielding a terrible sword with which to take the heads of his enemies, he was the antithesis of the drilled and disciplined soldiers of the hoplite phalanx and Roman cohort. This book is about the life of such a Celtic warrior, his place in Celtic society and how he lived, fought and died.

The Gundestrup Cauldron was discovered in a peat bog in Denmark and was probably a votive offering. It has many Celtic features, but it is probably not Celtic in origin. The exotic animal motifs suggest oriental influence. It is now believed to have been made in the lower Danube region, in Dacia or Thrace (modern Romania and Bulgaria). (The National Museum of Denmark)

Who were the Celts?

In the 5th century BC the Greek writer Ephoros described the Celts as one of the four great barbarian peoples, together with the Scythians, the Persians and the Libyans, who lived beyond the confines of the Classical Mediterranean world. They were called *Keltoi* or *Galatae* by the Greeks and either *Celtae* or *Galli* by the Romans. Their homeland was known to lie north of the Alps. Documentary and archaeological evidence suggests that by 500 BC the Celts occupied lands stretching from the Iberian Peninsula to the upper Danube. We do not know whether the peoples whom we now refer to as the Celts knew themselves by this

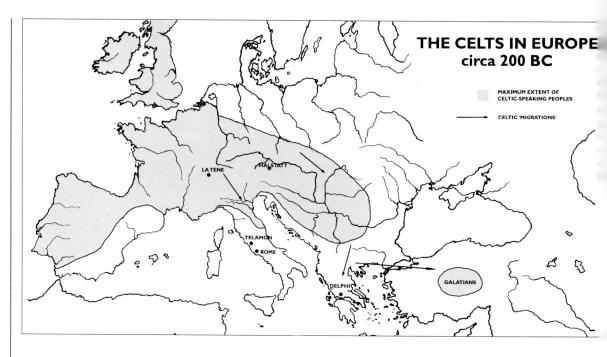

Map: The Celts in Europe.

name, nor do we know whether they had any concept of a common identity beyond that of the tribe. They certainly had much in common in terms of material culture, social structure and religious belief, but at the same time they exhibited great variety. Although still the subject of academic debate, the most satisfactory definition of the Celts for our purposes here is:

> 'Those peoples living in central and western Europe during the latter half of the first millennium BC and speaking dialects of the Indo-European language family now known as Celtic.'

Sources of evidence

Our knowledge of the Celts and their world comes from a variety of sources. All the evidence is indirect since Celtic society was almost entirely non-literate. With the exception of a number of funerary inscriptions and other items from southern France and Spain, the Celts have left no written records. There are three main categories of evidence: the accounts of Greek and Roman writers such as Polybius, Diodorus Siculus, Caesar and Livy; the later vernacular literature of surviving Celtic societies in the post-Roman period; and material remains revealed by modern archaeological excavation. Each of these sources has its shortcomings. The works of classical authors have the advantage of being contemporary with their subject, but they suffer from inherent problems of bias, distortion and misunderstanding. They tended to stress the barbarian stereotype and to reflect what their audience expected to hear, that is that the Celts were a wild and savage people. Vernacular sources must also be treated with caution. Most were written down for the first time in the early Middle Ages in a Christian environment, and are all solely concerned with the myths and legends of Wales and Ireland, countries that lay at the very edge of the Celtic world in the pre-Roman period. Although on its own archaeology can

provide, at best, only a partial picture, its great strength lies in the fact that it is free from the prejudice of classical commentators and medieval copyists (though not always from archaeologists). Nevertheless, when considered together, these three sources of evidence enable us to compile a plausible view of the Celts and their world.

Historical outline

The earliest signs of a distinctive Celtic culture appear in the 6th century BC, towards the end of the Halstatt period of the European Iron Age. So-called after the site in Austria where excavations revealed a large number of rich burials, this period is characterised by the hill-fort settlements or 'princedoms' scattered across an area near the headwaters of several major rivers such as the Danube, the Rhine and the Saône. At the beginning of the 5th century BC the Halstatt princedoms were largely replaced by wealthy warrior societies further north, which extended from north-eastern France to Bohemia. Their

Great Roundhouse, Butser Ancient Farm: A modern reconstruction of the roundhouse typical of Celtic Britain before the Roman conquest. (Author's photograph)

material culture and artistic style, called La Tène after the site in Switzerland where it was first identified, has become synonymous with the Celts.

By about 400 BC, large numbers of Celts had begun to migrate from their homes north of the Alps. Possibly prompted by overpopulation, many thousands moved south into northern Italy to settle in the rich lands of the Po valley. They took over this region so completely that it became known as *Gallia Cisalpina* (Gaul on this side of the Alps). From there they continued to raid along the whole length of the peninsula, breaking the power of the Etruscan city-states and laying siege to Rome. The sack and burning of the city by the Celtic Gauls entailed consequences that endured for centuries. Out of their humiliation the Romans developed a fear and loathing of the Celts, the permanent barbarian threat from the north, which they dubbed the *terror Gallicus*. Other Celtic groups moved south-east along the Danube basin, the first steps on a journey that would take some of them through the Balkans, into Greece and across into Asia Minor. It is known that Alexander the Great established friendly relations with Celts in the Balkans before embarking upon his campaigns in Asia, and that he received a Celtic delegation in Babylon after the defeat of the Persians. What encouraged the Celts to continue their mass migration into Macedonia in the early 3rd century BC is uncertain. Possibly it was the turmoil that followed the break-up of Alexander's empire. The Greek author Pausanias hints at this:

> 'It was then that Brennus strongly urged a campaign against Greece, enlarging on the weakness of Greece at the time, on the wealth of the Greek states and on the even greater wealth in the sanctuaries.'

Brennus won the argument and led his army to plunder Delphi, the greatest of all Greek sanctuaries. Shortly afterwards three Celtic tribes

Celtic society was predominantly rural. The vast majority of the population lived in small communities; large settlements were rare. (Copyright: P.J. Reynolds)

Round houses were characteristic of British Iron Age dwellings but were in contrast to their rectangular continental equivalents. This cut-away drawing is based on the reconstructed Great Roundhouse at Butser Ancient Farm in Hampshire. (Copyright: The British Museum)

crossed the Hellespont into Asia Minor where they settled in the area around what is now Ankara in Turkey.

The Celtic migrations to Italy and south-eastern Europe are well documented. In north-western Europe, and in particular the British Isles, the spread of La Tène culture in the 5th and 4th centuries BC was previously thought to be also the result of large-scale population movements. However, there is no archaeological evidence to support this, and it is now generally believed that Celtic-speaking peoples of the Atlantic seaboard gradually adopted the La Tène style to a greater or lesser extent through a process of cultural osmosis. By contrast, in the Iberian peninsula where the term 'Celt' is clearly recorded in the pre-Roman period, there was very little adoption of La Tène culture, a further indication that the Celtic world did not come about as the result of mass migration from a supposed homeland in central Europe. Hispanic Celtic speakers developed a close relationship with their Iberian neighbours producing the distinctive Celtiberian style.

The Celtic world reached its greatest extent at the beginning of the 3rd century BC. By the end of that century its power had begun to wane under pressure from Rome to the south and the gradual influx of Germanic peoples from the north. Cisalpine Gaul was the first to fall to Rome following the disastrous battle of Telamon. Victory over Carthage enabled the Romans to complete the subjugation of the Iberian peninsula. The creation of the 'Province' of *Gallia Transalpina* (Gaul on the far side of the Alps), at the end of the 2nd century BC made further intervention in Gaul inevitable. Caesar's campaigns devastated what had become the Celtic heartland. With Iberia almost entirely conquered, the Galatians in Asia Minor broken and the Danube now dominated by the Germans, the Romans turned to Britain. If invasion was a relatively easy matter, conquest was most certainly not. Finally, almost a century after they had landed, the Romans gave up their attempts to subdue the whole island. Hadrian built his wall to keep at bay 'the barbarian from the north', leaving Scotland and Ireland all that remained of a world that had lasted for more than five hundred years.

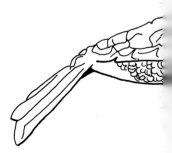

BELOW **Magnificent ceremonial helmet from Romania. The raven crest symbolises the Otherworldly power of the goddess of battle and death.**

CHRONOLOGY

BC

8th to 6th centuries: Early Iron Age Halstatt culture flourishes in west-central Europe.

c. 500: Decline of Halstatt princedoms and expansion of La Tène Iron Age cultures. 'Keltoi' first mentioned by the Greek author Ephoros.

c. 400: Beginning of 'Celtic Migrations'. The Boii, Cenomani, Lingones and Senones settle in the Po valley and on the Adriatic coast. Other Celtic-speaking tribes move south-east along the Danube valley. Decline of Etruscan power in northern Italy.

390 or 387: Celts sack Rome.

335 and 323: Alexander the Great receives Celtic delegations in the Balkans and in Babylon.

279: Celts invade Macedonia. Victory over the Greeks at Thermopylae. The Celts go on to sack the sanctuary at Delphi but are defeated in battle.

278: The Celtic Tectosages, Trocmii and Tolistobogii cross into Asia Minor.

277: Celts defeated at Lysimachia, ending the threat to Greece.

275: Celtic Galatians defeated by Antiochus of Seleucia.

240: Galatians defeated by Attalus of Pergamon.

225: Celts defeated by Rome at Telamon. Decline of Celtic power in northern Italy, leading to the creation of the Roman province of Gallia Cisalpina.

218–202: Second Punic War. Celtiberian and Gallic mercenaries play a major role in Carthaginian victories over Rome.

197–179 and 154–133: Rome attempts to subdue the Celtiberian tribes in Iberia.

133: Celtiberian resistance broken at the siege of Numantia.

125: Rome intervenes on behalf of Massalia (Marseille) against the Gallic Saluvii. Beginning of Roman military intervention in Gaul.

124–121: Defeat of the Saluvii, Allobroges and Arverni by Rome. Foundation of the Roman military base at Aquae Sextiae (Aix-en-Provence).

118: Creation of the Roman Province of Gallia Transalpina.

112–101: Migration through Gaul of the Cimbri and Teutones, a mix of Celtic and Germanic peoples from northern Europe. After several victories over the Romans they are finally defeated by Marius at Aquae Sextiae in 102 and Vercellae in 101.

88–66: Galatians fight as allies of Rome in its war against Mithridates IV of Pontus.

64: Galatia becomes a client state of Rome. Deiotarus of the Tolistobogii becomes pre-eminent leader of the Galatae under the patronage of Pompey.

60: Celtic Boii in Bohemia defeated by Dacian tribes from the lower Danube.

58–51: Caesar's campaigns in Gaul ending in the complete subjugation of the Gauls to Rome.

55 and 54: Reconnaissance in force by Caesar into south-eastern Britain.

52: Siege of Alesia. Surrender of Vercingetorix.

21: Sacrovir's rebellion in Gaul.

AD

43: Roman invasion of southern Britain. British resistance led by Caratacus until betrayed in 52 by Cartimandua, Queen of the Brigantes.

RIGHT **The richly decorated Deskborough Mirror, with its chased and engraved abstract patterns, is a fine example of Celtic art and metalwork. The plain bronze face would have been highly polished. (Copyright: The British Museum)**

60: Boudicca's rebellion.

70s: Subjugation of northern Britain.

84: Agricola defeats the Caledones at the battle of Mons Graupius.

86–87: Roman withdrawal from southern Caledonia.

122: Hadrian visits Britain.

122–138: Construction of Hadrian's Wall and its associated forts.

THE WARRIOR IN CELTIC SOCIETY

Celtic society, both before and after the Roman period, has often been described as 'heroic', dominated by a warrior elite whose lives were spent in an environment of perpetual conflict. Rich grave goods, including weapons and armour, together with later myths and legends

Torcs were worn by high status nobles and warriors as a sign of their rank. It is probable that the torc also possessed a religious and/or ritual symbolism. This example is made from an alloy of gold, silver and copper and has a diameter of 19.5cms (7¹⁄₂ins). (Copyright: The British Museum)

This bronze flagon from Lorraine, France, is one of a virtually identical pair, decorated with coral and red enamel. Dated to c. 400 BC, flagons such as these were modelled on far simpler Etruscan jars. Note the allusion to hunting and sport, an indication that such objects were for aristocratic use. (Copyright: The British Museum)

have reinforced this image. However, in recent years this view has come under increasing criticism from British archaeologists, many of whom now consider that the overwhelming majority of the population of Iron Age Europe was far more concerned with the plough than the sword. This may well be the case, but it is perhaps a little disingenuous to assume that the one necessarily precludes the other. Caesar's commentaries, though doubtless tailored to his own political purposes, reveal a world in which warfare was endemic. Moreover, as we shall see, warfare and conflict played an essential part in the maintenance of the very structure of Celtic society itself.

The structure of society

At the lowest level, Celtic society was made up of extended families or clans that were grouped together to form territorially based tribes. These were usually governed by a king or high chief, often in pairs, although by the mid-1st century BC some tribes in Gaul were ruled by elected 'magistrates', in many ways comparable to the consuls of the Roman Republic. Magistrates had only limited power. Most decisions were taken, or at least endorsed by a popular assembly of all the free men of the tribe. Real power lay with a smaller council of leading nobles among whom kings and chieftains were chosen.

A child born in Gaul or southern Britain towards the end of the pre-Roman Iron Age grew up in a society that possessed a very clear and strict hierarchy. Caesar was oversimplifying matters, however, when he said that:

'In Gaul there are only two classes of men who are of any account or consideration. The common people are treated almost as slaves . . . The two privileged classes are the Druids and the nobles.'

Although we know very little about the mass of common people through classical texts, they were not slaves. Slavery certainly existed but to a far lesser extent than in the 'civilised' Mediterranean world. Yet,

Plain and decorated torcs from a horde discovered at Ipswich. (Copyright: The British Museum)

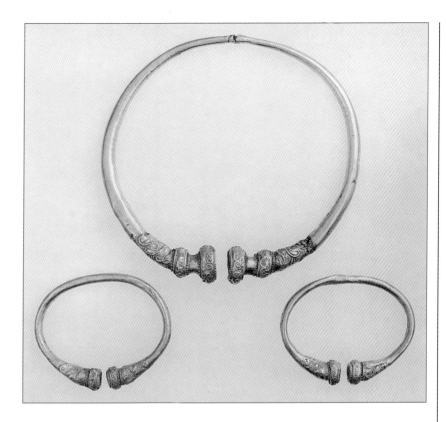

slave raiding was one of the principal motives for Celtic warfare. The captives were used as a trading commodity in exchange for luxury goods from Greece and Rome.

The Druids formed part of the privileged class known in Ireland as 'men of art', which also included bards, who extolled the warrior hero in song. Artisans, especially blacksmiths and other metalworkers, who manufactured not only everyday tools but also much of the finery – weapons and jewellery – worn by the Celtic nobles to emphasise their wealth and rank, were also regarded as men of art. Polybius wrote of the Gauls in northern Italy:

'Their possessions consist of cattle and gold because these were the only things they could carry about with them everywhere according to circumstance.'

The role of the Celtic noble was to wage war and in so doing increase his personal reputation in the eyes of his peers. Caesar wrote:

'Whenever war breaks out and their services are required . . . they all take the field, surrounded by their retainers and dependants of whom each noble has a greater or smaller number according to his birth and fortune. The possession of such a following is the only criterion of influence and power that they recognise.'

Clientage

This threefold division of Celtic society was therefore interdependent, each part supporting and supported by the other two. Society was held

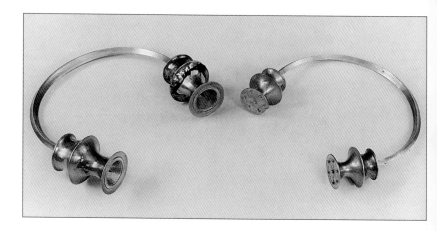

These torcs with unusual 'hour glass' terminals were discovered in Orense in northern Spain. (Copyright: The British Museum)

together by a complex web of family ties and other obligations, within which the warrior noble strove to attain wealth and prestige. Wealth came from agriculture, distribution of foreign luxury goods and success in war. From wealth came prestige, renown and power.

According to Polybius:

'They treated comradeship as of the greatest importance, those among them being the most feared and most powerful who were thought to have the largest number of attendants and associates.'

Having a large retinue of attendants or clients was a reflection of one's standing in society. Clientage was an agreement of mutual obligation by which the lower ranking would pledge allegiance to the higher in return for security, patronage and employment. Thus, the common people, the unfree, would serve with their labour the free men of the tribe, those entitled to attend the popular assembly. The free men would in turn support the nobility in peace and above all in war. It was an agreement closely bound up with personal honour, and which had dire consequences for any who did not respect their obligations. Clientage could also extend to other tribes and even between tribes themselves: for example, the rival Aedui and Sequani and their respective client tribes in Gaul at the time of

Italian wine was exported in amphorae such as this throughout Gaul and beyond. Its redistribution was controlled by local Celtic nobility who enhanced their status by extravagant displays of public generosity. The price paid was said to be one slave per amphora of wine. (Copyright: The British Museum)

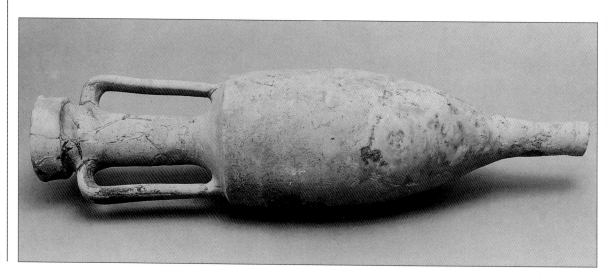

Caesar's campaigns. However, this continual competition for wealth, power and influence gave rise to a hierarchy that was inherently unstable. Freemen could, in the right circumstances, aspire to noble status, while some nobles such as Dumnorix and Orgetorix during the Gallic War had such powerful personal followings that they posed a threat to the stability of the tribe itself.

Clientage was often reinforced by the exchange of hostages or the fostering of children in the household of a patron. In the epic Irish tale *Táin Bo Cuailnge* (The Cattle Raid of Cooley), which is commonly called 'The Táin', the new-born hero Cúchulainn is given into the care not only of his aunt (the sister of his father the king) but also of the king's closest retainers in order that: 'In this manner he will be formed by all – chariot warrior, prince and sage.'

The legend of King Arthur also tells of how the young prince Arthur was brought up in secret in the household of Sir Ector with his foster brother Cai, a relationship that was often far stronger than ties of blood in Celtic society.

Given the significance of the number seven in Celtic myth, childhood was probably the first seven years of life. Boys reached manhood with, according to their social rank, the right to bear arms at 14, while girls were regarded as eligible for marriage at the same age. For young nobles and sons of freemen who had been fostered, reaching 14 meant it was time to become the client of a famous lord or attempt to attract a following of their own. In Ireland, such warrior retinues were called *fianna* and in Wales, *cantrefs*. Junior warriors would have sought to follow experienced warriors whose success would bring a greater chance of wealth and glory. See the diagram on the dynamics of the raid and the relevant section on pp. 14 and 17 for further reference.

Status

Cattle-reiving, slave raiding and vendettas between clans and tribes formed the basis of a low-intensity warfare that permeated Celtic society.

Finely worked goblets used in the consumption of highly valued Italian wine. Vessels such as these were based on Etruscan designs; however, Celtic craftsmen would have developed and embellished their work to surpass the originals. (Copyright: The British Museum)

The presence of the iron frame and fire dogs among grave goods stresses the importance of the feast even after death. The frame would have held the ritual cauldron over the fire. Note the stylised animal heads. Cattle were regarded as a mark of wealth in Celtic society. (Copyright: The British Museum)

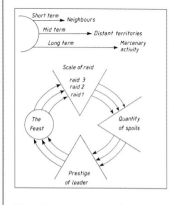

The raid was an essential part of the structure of Celtic society and of the warrior's place within it. (After Cunliffe)

Such conflicts provided a starting point for the young warrior, giving him the opportunity to demonstrate his bravery and skill at weapon-handling. But in a society that took personal courage for granted, something more was required in order to establish a reputation.

Celtic warriors served as mercenaries in many armies of the classical period. The best known Celtic mercenaries were those who joined Hannibal in his invasion of Italy during the Second Punic War, and who contributed to his victories against Rome at Lake Trasimene and Cannae. Celts also fought in the armies of Syracuse and the Successor kingdoms that followed the break-up of Alexander's empire in Egypt and the Levant, and later as auxiliaries in the Roman army itself. Clearly, many Celts looked for fame and fortune in the rich, exotic Mediterranean world, in the hope of returning home with their reputations made. Mercenary services also helped to reduce social pressure by removing numbers of young warriors from their tribes at a time when their drive to achieve high status was at its most intense.

This may explain the reference by Polybius to the large group of Celtic mercenaries who came south over the Alps to fight with the Cisalpine Gauls against the Romans at the battle of Telamon. Polybius called them *Gaesatae* which is more usually translated as 'spearmen' after the Celtic word *gaesum* (which means spear). Their organisation and

The powerful image of *Cernunnos* (the horned man), was common in Gaul. It suggests a symbolic union between man and the creatures of the wild, in particular the stag, which was widely venerated for its strength and virility. The torc is clearly shown to be a ritual object and it is perhaps significant that the main figure clutches a serpent in its left hand, another symbol of fertility and regeneration. (The National Museum of Denmark)

esprit de corps indicates that such Celtic mercenary warriors formed a distinct group outside the normal social structure of the clan and tribe. The Celtic word *geissi* (which means bonds, taboos or sacred rules of conduct) may shed some light here. The spiritual aspects of the warrior's life will be examined in more detail below. It is clear, however, that the custom of the Gaesatae, and on occasions of other Celtic warriors, to appear naked on the field of battle can be interpreted as a ritual action.

To maintain and enhance status required wealth and prestige. Once again, the riches of Greece and Rome offered a solution. Trade with the Mediterranean had a significant impact on the Celtic world. Changes in trading patterns were a factor in the decline of the Halstatt princedoms and the subsequent expansion of La Tène culture. Control of imported luxury goods, especially gold coins and Italian wine, was guaranteed to attract a large following and lay, inevitably, in the hands of the nobility. Warriors and other clients were rewarded with foreign luxuries, the value of which was measured by the influence it could command in being given away. This method of redistributing prestige items to increase status, called *potlach*, explains the incredulity of Diodorus Siculus when he wrote:

'The Gauls are exceedingly addicted to wine . . . brought into their country by merchants [who] receive an incredible price for it: a slave in exchange for a jar of wine.'

The Roman merchant doubtless believed that he was getting the best of the bargain. But the Celtic noble knew the value of the deal. Slaves were easy to obtain, while dispensing the wine freely would reinforce his standing in the tribe as a man of substance and largesse, whom others would wish to follow and share in his wealth. Poseidonius tells of Lovernius who:

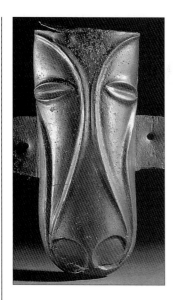

Found in a hoard at Stanwick, North Yorkshire, and possibly intended to decorate a chariot, this bronze horse-head mask, formed from simple abstract lines, presents a further example of the reverence in which this particular animal was held by the Celts. (Copyright: The British Museum)

'. . . in an attempt to win popular favour rode across the country in a chariot distributing gold and silver to [those] who followed him. Moreover, he set up a square enclosure one and a half miles on each side within which he filled vats with expensive liquor and prepared so great a quantity of food that for many days all who wished could come and enjoy the feast.'

The feast

Feasts were important social gatherings, usually wild and drunken, sometimes even deadly, and often with ritual significance. A strict ceremonial was observed with regard to precedence and hospitality. Seating was arranged according to rank and prowess. Poseidonius wrote:

'. . . they sit in a circle with the most influential man in the centre whether he be the greatest in warlike skill, nobility of family or wealth. Beside him sits the host and on either side of them the others in order of distinction. Their shield bearers stand behind them while their spearmen are seated on the opposite side and feast in common like their lords.'

Also in attendance were bards, who would celebrate the lineage, bravery and wealth of their patrons. Their songs, however, could either praise or satirise, and fear of losing face in front of their guests encouraged Celtic nobles and warriors to be even more generous than usual. Poseidonius continues with the tale of Lovernius:

'A poet who arrived too late met Lovernius and composed a song praising his greatness and lamenting his own late arrival. Lovernius threw a bag of gold to the bard who ran beside his chariot and sang another song saying that the very tracks gave gold and largesse.'

Strangers were allowed to share the meal before being asked their name and business. Everyone had a joint of meat according to their status. Traditionally, the greatest warrior received the choicest cut, the champion's portion of the thigh piece. It was a moment when any other

The boars are probably helmet crests rather than free-standing figures. The wheel was a common symbol of the sun, and it was often worn by the warrior as a protective amulet. Length of left-hand boar: 8.5cms (3½ins). (Copyright: The British Museum)

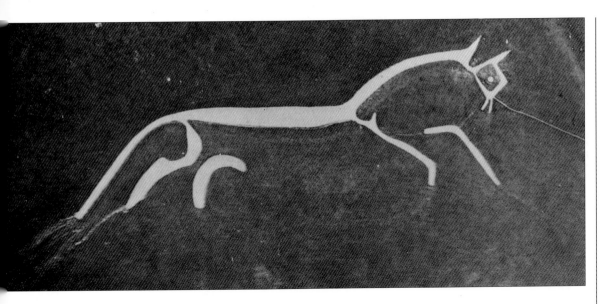

warrior had the right to dispute his position and challenge him. Others sought to reinforce their status in a rough-and-tumble that often escalated into more serious violence. Poseidonius again:

> 'The Celts sometimes engage in single combat at dinner. Assembling in arms they engage in a mock battle drill and mutual thrust and parry. Sometimes wounds are inflicted, and the irritation caused by this may even lead to the killing of the opponent unless they are held back by their friends . . . When the hindquarters were served up, the bravest hero took the thigh piece; if another man claimed it they stood up and fought in single combat to the death.'

The ultimate gesture in this desire for status was the death pact. Poseidonius describes a typical pact made at a feast:

> 'Others in the presence of the assembly received silver or gold or a certain number of jars of wine and, having taken pledges of the gift and distributed it among their friends and kin, lay stretched out face upwards on their shields. Another standing by cut his throat with his sword.'

The raid

Amidst the drinking, boasting and singing, a warrior might propose to lead a raid and would encourage others to join him, tempting them with the prospect of loot and glory. The number of warriors who agreed to follow was determined by the leader's status. The more volunteers he could recruit, the greater the chance of a successful outcome. A raid that brought spoils for him to distribute among his retinue would enhance his status as a leader. On a future occasion he would be able to attract a larger following, which in turn would have higher expectations of success and loot to be gained. Initially, younger warriors competed with each other but, once they had experienced initial success, they would dare to challenge their elders too. Small-scale raids

Stylised horse cut into the chalk at Uffington in Berkshire. Although Epona the horse goddess was not as widely revered in Britain as in Gaul, could this imposing figure symbolise the guardian spirit of the Belgae? (Copyright: The British Museum)

Silver coin from Slovakia. Both the horse and the wheel were symbols of the sun god in Celtic mythology. (After Duval)

17

on neighbouring clans to reive a few head of cattle would grow into inter-tribal conflicts and wider raiding over longer distances. Groups of warriors fighting as mercenaries in foreign armies was a logical step in this process. Once established, the cycle of conflict fed on itself and became essential to the maintenance of the structure of Celtic society.

The Otherworld

Ritual and spiritual belief pervaded all aspects of the warrior's life. The supernatural was all around him: every tree and river, mountain and spring was imbued with its own particular spirit. Trees and watercourses were held to be especially sacred. The most important ceremonies took place within sacred groves of oak trees called *drunemeton* (oak sanctuary to the Galatae of Asia Minor), while rivers, lakes and bogs across Europe have revealed ritual objects ranging from weapons and jewellery to animal and human sacrifices. Birds and animals held special significance too. Certain creatures were revered by the warrior for specific qualities, such as valour, speed, ferocity and fidelity. Most commonly regarded as revered were the horse, the bull, the wild boar, the raven and the dog. By adopting the symbol, on clothing or armour, and also in appearance, and by invoking the spirit of a particular animal, the warrior believed that he would be granted the same qualities as the revered beast.

The everyday world of men and the Otherworld of the gods and the dead existed side by side. The line dividing one from the other was often blurred and ill defined. Neither was there any firm boundary between human and animal form. The story of the warrior hero who strays unwittingly into the Otherworld while pursuing some enchanted beast is a common theme in Welsh and Irish legend. Linking the two worlds stood the Druids, whose name is cognate with the Celtic word for oak. Known definitely only in Britain and Gaul, it is nevertheless more than likely that an equivalent class existed throughout the Celtic world. The Galatians, for example, had judges who assisted the tribal leaders. Druids enjoyed high status as the guardians of tribal tradition, as administrators of tribal law and as mediators with the gods. Their main role was to interpret and control supernatural forces by means of divination. Caesar wrote:

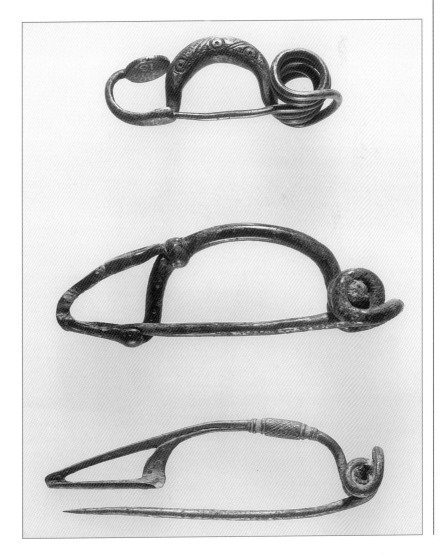

Early La Tène bronze brooches. Often highly decorated, they acted like a modern safety pin. (Copyright: The British Museum)

Statue dating from the 1st century BC. The characteristic mail-shirt, torc and sword-belt of the Celtic warrior are clearly shown. However, the subject's short hair and lack of moustache and beard might suggest a Gaul in Roman service or a Roman officer of a native auxiliary unit. (Musée Calvet, Avignon)

'The Druids officiate at the worship of the gods, regulate public and private sacrifice, and rule on all religious questions.'

Druid authority was both spiritual and civil, and extended from individuals to whole tribes. Anyone foolhardy enough to defy or disregard a Druid's ruling was excommunicated, debarred from taking part in sacrifice: according to Caesar the heaviest punishment that could be inflicted on a Gaul. Such individuals were shunned by others as unclean. Druids were almost certainly responsible for the imposition of *geissi* (taboos) on a warrior and for overseeing the taking of oaths.

APPEARANCE, DRESS AND EQUIPMENT

Appearance

Both on the field of battle and away from it, the Celtic warrior sought to demonstrate his wealth and status in his appearance and by the quality of his dress and equipment. To the Greeks and Romans, more used to darker hair and complexions, fair-haired Celts seemed strange and outlandish. Diodorus Siculus describes them at some length:

'The Gauls are tall of body, with rippling muscles, and white of skin. Their hair is fair, not only by nature but also because of their custom of accentuating it by artificial means. They wash their hair in lime-water then pull it back so that it differs little from a horse's mane. Some of them shave their beard, others let it grow. The nobles shave their cheeks but let their moustache grow until it covers their mouth.'

Despite their reputation for being tall, archaeological remains seem to indicate that the average height for a man was 1.7m (5ft 7ins). The average height for Romans, however, was several centimetres smaller. The reference to lime-washed hair is interesting in the light of the spiritual symbolism of the horse, and such hair was probably worn by warriors who had adopted the animal as their totem, thus invoking the protection of Epona, the horse goddess. Lime-washing had a practical benefit as well, since the process coarsened and stiffened the hair, providing a degree of protection from blows to the head. The disadvantage was that repeated application caused burning to the scalp and the hair to fall out. It was also difficult for the warrior to wear a helmet with lime-washed hair, although it is unlikely that a Celt would have desired or felt the need to do so, believing himself to be adequately protected by his totem.

Warriors in Britain presented an even stranger spectacle due to their habit of painting or tattooing their bodies with woad, a plant from which a deep blue dye was extracted. Similar customs have been observed in many cultures and, as well as indicating social rank, almost invariably have a ritual significance. The individual is again protected and his strength enhanced by the sacred symbolism of the swirling forms on his face, arms and torso.

Dress

Diodorus Siculus had this to say about they way the Celts dressed:

'The clothing they wear is striking – tunics which have been dyed and embroidered in various colours, and breeches; they also wear striped cloaks fastened by a brooch on the shoulder, heavy for winter and light for summer, in which are set checks, close together and of various hues.'

From contemporary descriptions and from the fragments of textiles recovered from graves a fair idea may be gained of the clothes worn by the Celtic warrior. Most items were colourful, well made and of wool or linen. The highest status nobles, whose clothes were often embroidered with gold thread, also wore some silk. The reference to close-set, variegated checks brings to mind the tweed or tartan-like designs of a later age. Colours, however bright when new, would fade quickly because of the vegetable dyes used.

Celtic love of display and ornament was emphasised by the jewellery worn by the warrior to announce his wealth and status. Diodorus Siculus again:

'They amass a great quantity of gold which is used for ornament not only by the women but also by the men. They wear bracelets on their wrists and arms, and heavy necklaces of solid gold, rings of great value and even gold corselets.'

Of all the Celtic jewellery, the most impressive in the eyes of Mediterranean commentators was the neck-ring, or 'torc'. To the Romans it characterised the Celtic warrior although it was not unique to the Celts. The torc could be of gold, bronze or iron according to the wealth of the wearer. It is quite possible that it possessed a symbolic significance since not all were made of precious metal. It was almost

This section of the Gundestrup Cauldron portrays both mounted warriors and warriors on foot. None of the latter wear helmets except the figure on the right, seemingly armed with a sword, who appears to be the leader. Helmet crests on this figure and on the horsemen suggest animal totems: boar, raven, stag, bull and horse. The Celtic war horn, the Carnyx, is clearly shown. But what are we to make of the figure on the left? Could it be a representation of rebirth via the symbolism of the cauldron itself, shown here, after death on the battlefield? (The National Museum of Denmark)

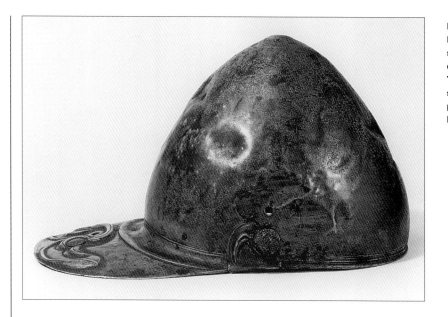

certainly an indication of rank (the Gauls presented a golden torc to the Emperor Augustus supposedly 45 kg [100lbs] in weight), with perhaps in some cases ritual or religious overtones. Many representations of Celtic deities are portrayed wearing the torc.

Arms and equipment

The bearing of arms was the right and duty of every free man in Celtic society and served to differentiate him, immediately and clearly, from the unfree majority. The basic panoply of the Celtic warrior was the spear and shield. To this he could add the sword and, for the nobility or as wealth and status permitted, a helmet and possibly a mail-shirt. Diodorus Siculus provides a detailed description:

'Their arms include man-sized shields decorated according to individual taste. Some of these have projecting figures in bronze skilfully made not only for decoration but also for protection. They wear bronze helmets with large figures, which give the wearer the appearance of enormous size. In some cases horns are attached, in others the foreparts of birds or beasts . . . Some of them have iron breastplates or chainmail while others fight naked. They carry long swords held by a chain of bronze or iron hanging on their right side . . . They brandish spears which have iron heads a cubit or more in length and a little less than two palms in breadth. Some are forged straight, others are twisted so that the blow does not merely cut the flesh but in withdrawing will lacerate the wound.'

The spear was the primary weapon and symbol of the warrior. The Greek writer Strabo commented that the Celtic warrior carried two types of spear: a larger, heavier one for thrusting; and a smaller, lighter javelin that could be both thrown and used at close quarters.

Pausanias, writing of the Galatae, remarked that their only defensive armour were their national shields. From this we may infer that mail-shirts were not worn even by Galatian nobles and that the shape of

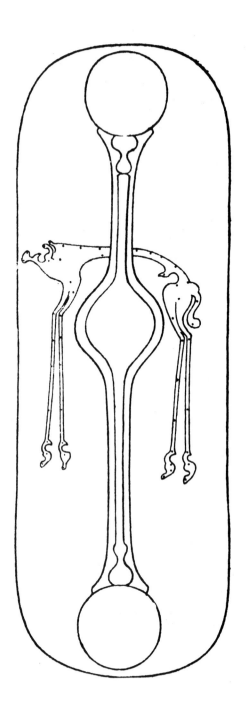

ABOVE LEFT **The Witham Shield, recovered from the river of the same name in Lincolnshire is interesting not only because of its ceremonial nature but also because of its offset boss and the very faint outline of a stylised boar, which was originally riveted to the bronze face of the shield. (Copyright: The British Museum)**

ABOVE RIGHT **Artist's impression of the appearance of the bronze boar riveted to the face of the Witham Shield. It is likely that other Celtic shields were decorated in a similar, though simpler manner, with animal totems painted on. (Copyright: The British Museum)**

23

their shields was distinctive to Greek eyes. According to Livy, Galatian shields were 'long and oblong', a description backed up by archaeological finds.

The sword was the weapon of the high status warrior. To carry one was to display a symbol of status and prestige. For this reason, many swords and scabbards were elaborately decorated with precious metals and stones. Traditional Irish tales speak of gold- and ivory-hilted swords. Archaeological evidence has proved that Celtic swords were of high quality, flexible and with a sharp, strong cutting edge, contradicting Polybius' comments that in battle the blade quickly became so bent that the warrior had to straighten it with his foot. Confusion probably arose over the practice of ritually 'killing' a sword by deliberately bending it as part of a burial ceremony or sacrifice to the gods.

Helmets were a rare sight among Celtic warriors; worn only by those whose wealth and prestige permitted them to flaunt their status. Many helmets were intended more for display than for war, as shown by the discovery of elaborate examples such as the horned Waterloo Helmet and the magnificent specimen from Ciumesti in Romania, found complete with its articulated raven crest. The representation of specific animals and birds reminds us of the mystic symbolism that such creatures held for the warrior and the supernatural power that they conferred.

Mail-shirts were an even rarer sight on the battlefield than helmets. They were worn only by noble warriors of the very highest status. Remnants of iron mail appear for the first time in graves dating from the early 3rd century BC, and it is believed that it was first invented by Celtic blacksmiths sometime before 300 BC.

Neither the bow nor the sling featured greatly among the weapons of the Celtic warrior, though both were used to some extent in Celtic warfare. For the former, there is very little archaeological evidence, although some iron arrowheads have been discovered at the site of Alesia

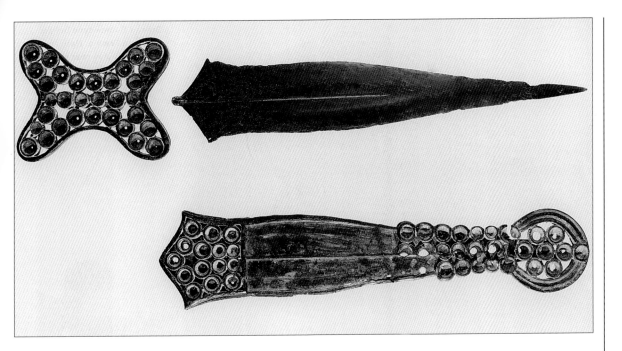

This iron leaf-shaped dagger and its sheath would have been elaborately decorated with coloured glass, enamel or perhaps coral. (Copyright: The British Museum)

LEFT The sword was the weapon of the noble warrior. This unique example from Kirkburn, Yorkshire, has scarlet enamel on the hilt and scabbard, and is a tribute to the workmanship of the Celtic swordsmith. (Copyright: The British Museum)

in Gaul. For the latter, however, there is ample evidence. Vast stockpiles of slingstones have been unearthed within several of the hill-forts in southern Britain, a clear indication that their use was a major factor in the defence of these sites. It has been suggested that the elaborate arrangement of the ramparts at the entrances were specifically designed to maximise the effectiveness of this particular weapon. Nevertheless, the use of the sling is not mentioned in any set-piece battle.

An explanation is not difficult to find, bearing in mind the ethos of the warrior. Both the bow and the sling are missile weapons best employed at a distance from the enemy; they are also weapons of dissuasion. Arrows and slingstones can be directed towards an enemy, even in large volleys or showers, but they will not all find a target. Moreover, anyone can learn to use either weapon; they do not even have to use them particularly accurately to be effective. The Gallic leader Vercingetorix is reported to have called for all the archers who could be found in Gaul to be sent to him to make up for his losses after the siege of Avaricum. The implication here is that, despite the many thousands of warriors who were already fighting with him (according to Caesar over 250,000) these archers were not among them and might not otherwise have been expected to fight. Furthermore, the principal engagements following Avaricum were two other sieges, at Gergovia and the final defeat of the Gauls at Alesia. Vercingetorix used his archers to help defend his strongholds just as slingers defended British hill-forts.

The conclusion that has to be drawn is clear. The Celtic warrior used neither the bow nor the sling because they were not considered to be a warrior's weapons. His goal on the battlefield was to engage the enemy at close quarters with spear and sword, and to measure his prowess against that of his opponent in single combat. To stand off and shoot at him from a distance was unthinkable. Not to know who had vanquished whom, where was the honour in that?

THE FACE OF BATTLE

We have seen how warfare was endemic in Celtic society, how the warrior's desire for status and the dynamics of the raid brought him back time and again to the battlefield to prove himself in the eyes of his peers and his gods. Yet although the face of battle evolved rapidly as the Celtic and Mediterranean worlds came into conflict, the approach of the Celtic warrior towards it remained largely unchanged.

Polybius' account of the battle of Telamon describes some of the principal characteristics displayed by a Celtic army prior to engaging in a conflict:

'The Celts had deployed the Gaesatae from the Alps facing their rear, from where they expected [the Romans] to attack, and behind them the Insubres. Facing the opposite direction . . . they placed the Taurisci and the Boii . . . Their wagons and chariots they placed at the extremity of either wing, and collected their booty on a hill with a protecting force around it . . . The Insubres and Boii wore their breeches and light cloaks but the Gaesatae had discarded theirs owing to their proud confidence in themselves, and stood naked with nothing but their arms in front of the whole army . . . [The Romans] were terrified by the fine order of the Celtic host and the dreadful din, for there were numerous trumpeters and horn blowers, and the whole army was shouting its war cries at the same time. There was such a confused sound that the noise seemed to come not only from the trumpeters and warriors but also from the ground itself. No less terrifying were the appearance and gestures of the naked warriors in front, all of whom were finely built men in the prime of life, and all in the leading companies richly adorned with gold torcs and amulets.'

It is clear from this vivid extract that a Celtic host drawn up for battle presented an impressive and daunting sight to its opponent, as was the intention. Warriors wearing nothing but gold ornaments, the noise and sheer spectacle all served to reinforce the image of overwhelming power.

Deployment

Polybius' description also reveals that the deployment of a Celtic army on the field of battle was no mere 'column of mob'. Deployment was by tribal contingents. Within tribes, clans would deploy as separate entities, doubtless according to an acknowledged or perhaps traditional pecking order. The fianna would group themselves around the highest status warriors standing in the front line. The warriors' sense of pride and honour, which was easily offended, probably precluded any other option. Even an exceptionally gifted commander such as Vercingetorix had to operate within the accepted hierarchy. To identify each grouping in the battleline and to act as rallying points, the guardian deities of tribe and clan were carried into battle as standards topped with carved or cast figures of their animal forms. As with the eagles of Rome, these standards were religious symbols. Caesar describes the Gauls taking solemn vows before them.

Ritual nudity

Greeks and Romans were disconcerted to be faced with large numbers of Celtic warriors who fought completely naked. Yet the custom was not new and had been practised by the Greeks themselves in earlier times. Polybius attempted to rationalise it, saying that the Celts discarded their clothes because they considered that they would be a hindrance in the thorny, scrub-covered terrain at Telamon. There is in fact a practical aspect to it, as pieces of dirty cloth forced into a wound are difficult to extract and can lead to infection. Practicalities aside, other accounts speak of naked Celtic warriors at the battle of Cannae in 216 BC and in battles in Galatia a century later. What is interesting is that, in each instance, the Celts were fighting as mercenaries.

We have seen that Celtic mercenary warriors, sometimes referred to as Gaesatae, formed distinct groups outside the traditional social structure of the tribe or clan. The 'proud confidence in themselves', noted by Polybius may provide an explanation of why Celtic mercenaries had such a penchant for nudity in battle. First and foremost, it identified the individual warrior as a member of this select group. The warrior who chose to become a mercenary was bound by rules of conduct, taboos or geissi, other than those which governed his normal life within the clan. He would, at the very least, have dedicated himself to his fellow Gaesatae and very likely to a god of war, for example Camulos in Britain and Gaul. Thus, nudity on the battlefield assumes ritual significance. Protected and empowered by divine forces, the warrior displays his strength and perhaps his personal wealth also, and has no need for either armour or clothing. The fact that he carries a shield does not contradict the assumption of divine protection. The shield, like the spear and sword, was part of the warrior's panoply; it was not only his right but also his duty to bear them.

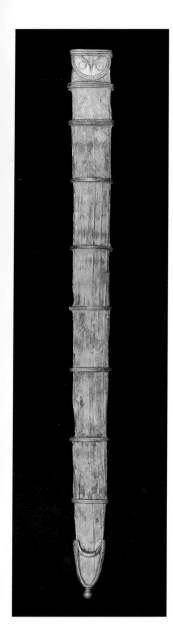

Sword scabbard made from ashwood and bound with bronze from Stanwick, Yorkshire. (Copyright: The British Museum)

Bronze fittings on a reconstructed shield. Note the bronze strip on the wooden spine and boss. Other small bronze discs were probably also fixed on the face of the shield. (Copyright: The British Museum)

Noise

As the Celtic host deployed for battle and caught sight of the enemy they set up a dreadful din. Each and every warrior gave full voice to his war cry or battle chant, doubtless mingled with taunts, insults and obscenities aimed at his opponent. To the cacophony of the warriors themselves was added the sound of the *carnyx* (war horn). Diodorus Siculus describes them in these terms:

'Their trumpets are of a peculiar kind: they blow into them and produce a harsh sound that suits the tumult of war.'

The carnyx was a long horn with a head and mouth in the form of an animal, often that of a wild boar. A particularly fine example in bronze was discovered at Deskford in Scotland in the early 19th century. It has been dated to the mid-1st century AD and is comparable with those featured on the Gundestrup Cauldron. When first excavated, the Deskford carnyx was found to have a wooden 'tongue' or clapper in the mouth, which probably increased the vibration of the braying, strident sound.

If the primary objective was to terrify and overawe his enemy, the Celtic warrior could justifiably claim that he succeeded. Polybius tells of the Romans' fear at Telamon. Describing the battle of Allia over 150 years earlier, just before the sack of Rome, Livy wrote of the Gauls:

'They are given to wild outbursts and they fill the air with hideous songs and varied cries.'

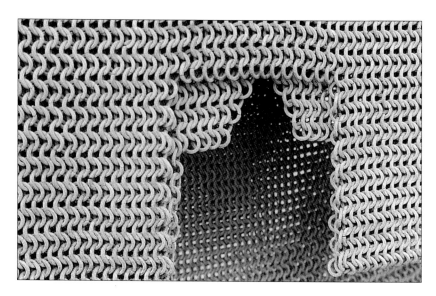

Modern reconstruction of a mail-shirt. The Celts are believed to have developed chain or ring mail in the late 4th century BC. (Author's photograph)

Bronze figurine of a naked Celtic warrior. The shield and spear or sword are lost, but the torc and sword belt are clearly visible. Note the horned helmet. Ritual nudity on the battlefield was a characteristic of the Gaesatae. (Staatliche Museum, Berlin)

Similarly, Livy wrote of the Galatae of Asia Minor:

'Their songs as they go into battle, their yells and leaping, and the dreadful noise of arms as they beat their shields in some ancestral custom – all this is done with one purpose: to terrify their enemies.'

The fear and dread described by Livy also filled Paulinus' army when it faced the British force, supported by Druids and 'banshee women' shouting and screaming awful curses while defending the Druids' 'holy of holies' on Anglesey in AD 59.

However, the Celtic war cry may have been more than a hideous cacophony intended to terrify opponents. We have already noted the importance to the warrior of certain creatures as totems and manifestations of divine power. Polybius' reference to the noise created by the Celtic host seeming to come 'also from the ground itself' could be interpreted as an attempt – conscious, or subconscious – to call upon the Otherworld forces immanent in the earth.

The effect of this sustained barrage of noise on the warrior himself was no less dramatic. In more modern terms, he became 'psyched up', working himself into a frenzy, often, it must be said, helped along by alcohol. He was convinced of his superiority through his utter belief in the power and protection of his guardian spirits. It only required a sign from the highest status leaders for the warrior to launch himself against the enemy. But before this, the greatest of these leaders, the heroes whose praises were sung at the feast, still had their own individual part to play in the ritual of battle.

29

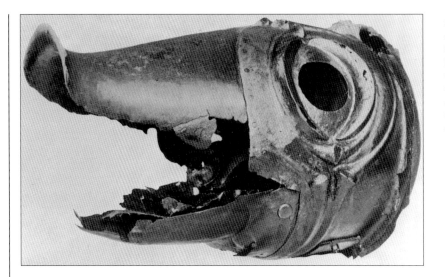

Single combat

As the opposing armies faced each other, prominent warriors would step forward and throw down a challenge. Diodorus Siculus says:

> 'When the armies are drawn up they are wont to advance in front of the line of battle and challenge the bravest of their opponents to single combat . . . When someone accepts the challenge, they recite the heroic deeds of their ancestors and proclaim their own valour, at the same time abusing and belittling their opponent in an attempt to rob him of his fighting spirit.'

Livy wrote of an incident when a Celtic warrior goaded a Roman into accepting his challenge by the simple expedient of poking his tongue out and laughing at him. The Roman had the last laugh, however, and killed his tormentor. On the point of robbing an enemy of his fighting spirit, in a similar confrontation, the extent of the warrior's faith in the power and favour of the gods is revealed by the utter collapse of the Celt's morale when a raven appeared to land on the Roman's helmet before flying threateningly towards the warrior. The will of the battle gods had been clearly demonstrated; resistance was useless and he was promptly despatched. In Irish myth, Badbh (the goddess of battle) and Morrigan (the Queen of Darkness) both manifested themselves as a raven or crow. The Táin tells of the death of Cúchulainn when both deities perched on his shoulder in the midst of battle, encouraging the men of Connacht to strike him down and take his head.

Battle frenzy and hand-to-hand combat

As the respective champions fought and either conquered or died in full view of their armies, tension rose to new heights. Then the clash of arms on shields, the braying of the carnyxes and the cries of 'Victory!' became a roar as one side saw their hero holding aloft his enemy's head. The warrior needed no further encouragement. The frenzy of battle was upon him and his enemy was there, momentarily stunned and disconcerted by the death of their man. Caesar wrote of the Gauls that it was a crime for clients to desert their patrons. To their own frenzy, therefore, was added the desire for revenge and they too launched themselves to the attack. The Táin contains a graphic description of the battle frenzy of the hero Cúchulainn:

'Then the frenzy of battle came upon him. You would have thought that every hair was being driven into his head, that every hair was tipped with a spark of fire. He closed one eye until it was no wider than the eye of a needle; he opened the other until it was as big as a wooden bowl. He bared his teeth from jaw to ear and opened his mouth until the gullet could be seen.'

The Celtic warrior used light javelins to throw and a heavier thrusting spear at close quarters. (Copyright: The British Museum)

ABOVE **Gold stater of the Atrebatic king Tincomarus, from a hoard found near Alton in Hampshire and featuring a highly stylised horse, a symbol of the Celtic sun god. (Copyright: The British Museum)**

RIGHT **The Celts were accomplished horsemen, and their mounted warriors were much sought after by the armies of Carthage and the Roman Republic. (Copyright: The British Museum)**

The ferocity of the Celtic charge was legendary. Caesar wrote of the Nervii at the battle of the Sambre during the Gallic War:

'. . . they suddenly dashed out in full force and swooped down on our cavalry which they easily routed. Then they ran down to the river at such an incredible speed that almost at the same moment they seemed to be at the edge of the forest, in the water and already upon us.'

Despite the mad rush of the warrior and his desire to close with his opponent, Tacitus, in his account of the battle of Mons Graupius, tells us that:

'The fighting began with an exchange of missiles. The Britons showed both steadiness and skill in parrying our spears with their huge swords or catching them on their little shields, while they themselves rained volleys on us.'

Having hurled his javelins at close range, the warrior battered his way into the enemy's ranks punching with his shield, thrusting with his spear

A: Gallic Noble Warrior, 1st century BC
(see plate commentary for full details)

A

B: The Battle of Telamon, 225 BC
(see plate commentary for full details)

B

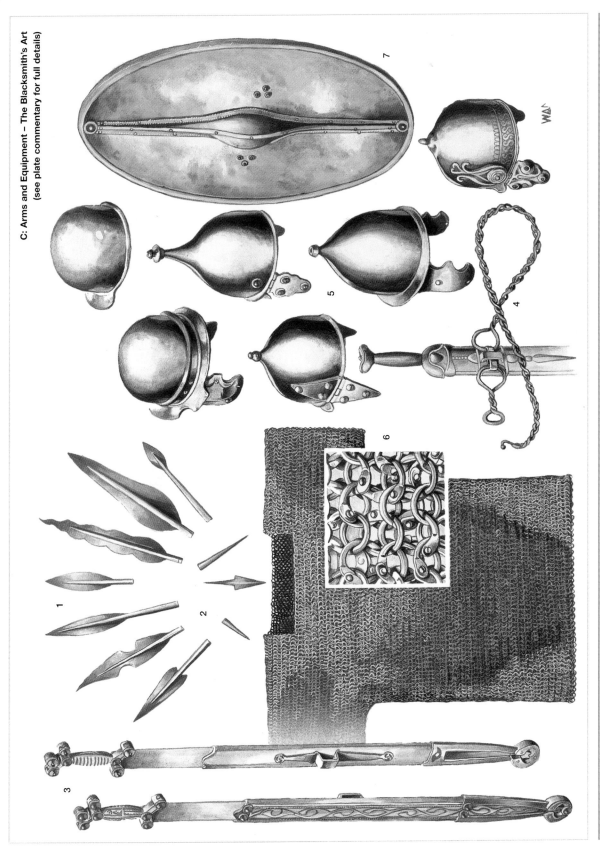

C: Arms and Equipment – The Blacksmith's Art
(see commentary for full details)

c

D: Fostering and Clientage, Southern Britain Early 1st century AD
(see plate commentary for full details)

D

E: Celtic Mounted Warrior, Italy 3rd century BC
(see plate commentary for full details)

E

F: Single Combat, Italy 3rd century BC
(see plate commentary for full details)

F

G: The Battle of the Sambre, 57 BC (see plate commentary for full details)

H: British Chariot Warrior, Early 1st century AD (see plate commentary for full details)

I: Ambush and Skirmish, Southern Britain mid 1st century B
(see plate commentary for full details)

J: The Spoils of War, Gaul early 1st century BC
(see plate commentary for full details)

J

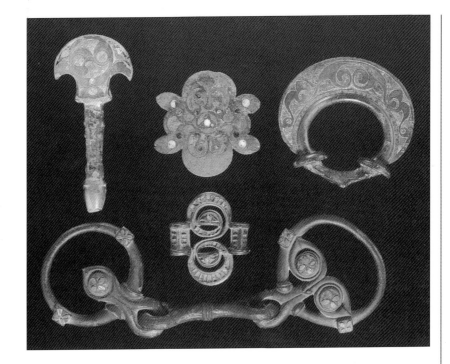

Horse and chariot harness fittings embellished with scrolls and geometric patterns in red, blue and yellow enamel. Height of top-left lynch pin 13.1cms (5ins). (Copyright: The British Museum)

or slashing with his sword. Against other Celts the battle was quickly transformed into a series of individual combats. The chaos and almost unimaginable bloodletting was portrayed by an unknown Irish author in the 9th century AD:

'Then the two armies made for each other. Fierce was the onslaught they made on either side. Bitter sights were seen there – the white fog of chalk and lime from the shields as they were struck by the edges of swords and the points of spears, which were skilfully

Chariot reconstruction based on archaeological finds, written descriptions and pictorial references. (Copyright: The British Museum)

parried by the heroes; the beating and shattering of the shield-bosses as they were belaboured with swords and stones; the noise of the pelting weapons; the gushing and shedding of blood and gore from the limbs of the champions and the sides of the warriors.'

The last phrase seems to reinforce the theory that the higher status warriors were armed with slashing swords whereas others fought with thrusting spears.

Against the disciplined close-order units of the armies of Greece and Rome, Celtic tactics were less successful. Breakthroughs were more difficult to achieve and neither cohort nor phalanx would obligingly disperse to engage in single combat. Caesar's references to the Gauls fighting in dense masses can be understood in these terms as they became stacked up against the Roman shield wall, the majority of them unable to come to grips. The type of weapons carried, the style of combat that they imposed, and the whole ethos of the Celtic warrior, all implied a looser order in battle.

By its very nature, the frenzied assault lacked all control. If the first mad rush failed to cause the enemy to flee or was unable to break his line, desperation soon began to set in. There was no way that hard-pressed troops could be withdrawn from the fight, and no reserve to bolster them. The warrior's code of honour made it impossible for him to stand back and watch others gain glory. For him, it was all or nothing. The fragility of Celtic armies and their lack of cohesion made for a fine line between success and failure. If one section of the battle line began to waiver it could cause uncertainty and even panic to spread quickly. Tacitus' account of the battle of Mons Graupius continued:

'On the British side each man now behaved according to his character. Whole groups, though they had weapons in their hands,

Celtic horse harness and chariot fittings were finely worked and decorated to stress the status of the warrior and the reverence of the horse as a living symbol of the sun god. Bit, lynch pins and terrets made from iron and bronze. (Copyright: The British Museum)

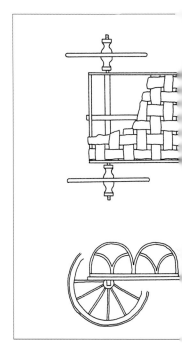

Hollow bronze chariot pole tips with incised ornamentation from Limerick, Republic of Ireland. (Copyright: The British Museum)

BELOW The light framework and the wicker or leather floor optimised the speed and manoeuvrability of a Celtic chariot, as shown by this reconstruction. (After Piggott)

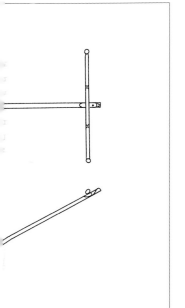

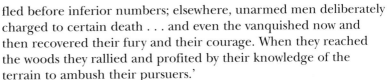

fled before inferior numbers; elsewhere, unarmed men deliberately charged to certain death . . . and even the vanquished now and then recovered their fury and their courage. When they reached the woods they rallied and profited by their knowledge of the terrain to ambush their pursuers.'

Nevertheless, we have several accounts of the determination of the Celtic warrior to carry on the fight to the death rather than run from the field. Caesar wrote of the Nervii:

'But the enemy, even in their desperate plight, showed such bravery that when their front ranks had fallen those immediately behind stood on their prostrate bodies to fight; and when these too fell and the corpses were piled high, the survivors still kept hurling javelins as though from the top of a mound, and flung back the spears they caught on their shields.'

Writing about the battle of Thermopylae over 200 years earlier, Pausanias remarked on the brutish 'fury and passion' of the Galatae which 'did not abate so long as life remained'.

The convictions that led the warrior to fight on and, seemingly, to embrace death are difficult for us to understand and appreciate. In the end it comes back to a question of personal honour, explicable in part by the close ties of mutual obligation between patron and client, and the obsessive desire of the warrior to gain prestige and stand well with his fellows, and perhaps also his foes.

The mounted warrior

Tacitus wrote that the main strength of the Celts lay in their infantry. However, they were also experienced in rearing and using horses, which were regarded as prestige animals and revered for their courage, speed

and sexual vigour. The animal was a symbol of the sun god, who was often portrayed as a horseman bearing a thunderbolt as a spear and the solar wheel as a shield. In Welsh myth, the hero Culwych appears as such in golden splendour at Arthur's court. The Irish horse goddess Macha was also a goddess of war, linked to Badbh and the Morrigan. Her name appears in Pausanias' reference to the method of fighting from horseback of the Galatae, called the *Trimarcisia*.

'To each horseman were attached two attendants who were themselves skilled riders. When the Galatian horsemen were engaged, these attendants remained behind the ranks. If the horseman was killed, one of the attendants would replace him; if injured, the second would help him back to camp. Should his horse be hurt, one of the attendants would bring him a remount.'

An indication of the effectiveness of this tactic is given by Caesar, who wrote:

'A further difficulty was that they never fought in close order, but in a very open formation, and had reserves posted here and there; in this way the various groups covered one another's retreat, and fresh troops replaced those that were tired.'

Decorative head, forming a handle mount, from a bronze-bound wooden bucket found among grave goods from a high status burial at Aylesford, Kent, England. This detail, taken from what was perhaps a ceremonial vessel, recalls the important symbolism of the human head in the Celtic belief system. (Copyright: The British Museum)

Vercingetorix himself led a group of Gallic cavalry together with light-armed warriors on foot at Avaricum to ambush Roman foragers. Such examples suggest that mounted Celtic warriors, almost certainly wealthy nobles of high status, engaged in battle in a manner that was more reminiscent of the heroic single combat than the mass brawl of the warrior on foot. The combination of light-armed infantry with skirmishing cavalry was a common enough practice, although for the Celts it was probably employed more in specific circumstances such as the ambush of an unsuspecting enemy rather than in open battle.

Celtic mercenary horsemen, especially the Gauls and Celtiberians, were much sought after, fighting for Hannibal in the Second Punic War and later on behalf of Rome when they provided Caesar with much of his mounted arm. The growing emphasis on cavalry among the Celts themselves from the end of the 3rd century BC can be seen in the increased length of sword blades, some reaching almost 90cms (35ins) in length. Such swords were too long to be easily wielded by an infantryman. Yet Pausanias speaks of Celts riding onto the battlefield and dismounting to engage the enemy, tethering their mounts by means of small pegs attached to the reins that they pushed into the ground. This may be an earlier custom in view of the tactics used by chariot warriors (see below) and the fact that Pausanias was writing of the time of the Celtic incursions into Greece and Asia Minor. The battle of

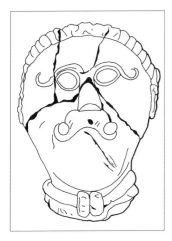

ABOVE **Stone head, perhaps of a Celtic god, found near a sanctuary in Bohemia. The Celts believed the head possessed great mystic significance to the warrior. Note the torc and the swept-back hair. (Norodni Museum, Prague)**

RIGHT **The human head possessed a mystic symbolism for the Celts, who believed that it was the dwelling-place of the soul. (Copyright: The British Museum)**

Telamon was a watershed insofar as it marked the last recorded large-scale use of chariots by Celtic armies in continental Europe, and in which Celtic cavalry played a major independent role.

The chariot warrior

Before the development of an effective cavalry arm, the Celtic warrior would often fight from a chariot. From the end of the 3rd century BC onwards chariots had fallen from use in continental Europe, so Caesar was surprised to find that they were still a major component of Celtic warfare at the time of his 'reconnaissance in force' into Britain 150 years later. He described the use of chariots in battle by the Britons at some length:

'In chariot fighting the Britons begin by driving all over the field hurling javelins. Generally, the terror inspired by the horses and the noise of the wheels are sufficient to throw their opponent's ranks into disorder. Then, after making their way between the squadrons of their own cavalry, they jump down from the chariots and engage on foot. In the meantime, the charioteers retire a short

47

Under 0.9m (3ft) long, the magnificent Battersea Shield recovered from the Thames is made of sheet bronze and is far too fragile to be used in war. A masterpiece of the Celtic metal worker's art, like the Waterloo Helmet, it was almost certainly a ceremonial item created especially as a gift to the gods. The panels are inlaid with red glass. (Copyright: The British Museum)

distance from the battle and place their vehicles in such a position that their masters, if hard pressed by numbers, have an easy means of retreat to their own lines. Thus, they combine the mobility of cavalry with the staying power of infantry.'

Caesar's account contains several interesting parallels with the behaviour of the warrior on foot and on horseback. The reference to the chariots driving about the battlefield recalls the intimidation of an opponent with noise and then the frenzied charge. Caesar wrote of the panic caused by chariots being driven at speed towards the Roman line, in which many were trampled underfoot. Similarly, the noble stepping

down to fight hand-to-hand after an exchange of missiles, while the chariot withdraws ready to pick him up again, brings to mind the Trimarcisia formation and tactic of the mounted warrior. The custom of single combat between nobles or heroes of near equal rank and status is also inferred. All in all, the impression is given of a style of combat better suited to the constant low-intensity warfare between clans or tribes than the 'total war' struggles against the Romans.

The idea of the joust is brought out in the Táin, together with the symbolism of the chariot, if anything stronger even than that of the horse. The wheel was widely depicted as an emblem of the sun god throughout Celtic Europe and beyond. The ritual aspect of combat between chariot warriors is clear from the following comment by the Queen of Tara's charioteer:

> ' Wait a minute . . . until I turn the chariot around to the right, with the sun, to draw down the power of the sign.'

Turning the chariot to the right, or clockwise, in the same way that the sun appears to circle the earth when looking towards it, would therefore invoke its Otherworldly power. At the same time, the warrior presented his shielded side to his opponent. To do so in full sight of the enemy could only be construed one way. Cúchulainn's charioteer, Loegh, says in an Irish tale from the 9th century:

> 'Here is the chariot back again, and it has turned its left side towards us.
> "That is an insult that cannot be endured," said Cúchulainn.'

Whatever the original tactics used, the effectiveness of the chariot against troops unused to it is evident from Caesar's description, especially when deployed in numbers (Cassivelaunus is said to have gathered four thousand at the battle of the Medway in 54 BC). This was due in no small measure to the skill of the charioteer. Caesar wrote that:

> ' . . . by daily training and practice they attain such proficiency that even on a steep slope they are able to control the horses at full gallop, and to check and turn them in a moment. They can run along the chariot pole, stand on the yoke and get back into the chariot as quick as lightning.'

Diodorus Siculus described charioteers as freemen, chosen by the nobles from the poorer classes, and employed also as shieldbearers. The relationship between the warrior and his charioteer was a particularly close one. The warrior effectively placed his life in the hands of his driver, whose skill and responsibility gave him his own unique status. The value placed upon the charioteer is apparently stressed in a 9th-century Irish manuscript that tells of a meeting between Cúchulainn and his enemy's charioteer. Despite his fearsome reputation, Cúchulainn reassures the other that 'he never kills charioteers'. Heroic exaggeration or an indication of a more general custom? The latter explanation is not so unlikely considering the emphasis upon single combat between warriors of similar rank. The charioteer, for all his skill, was chosen from a different social class. What honour and prestige was there to be gained by killing a man of lower status?

AFTERMATH

The warrior's attitude to death
From the accounts of Greek and Roman commentators highlighted above, it is obvious that the Celtic warrior had no fear of death in battle. This positive attitude is reinforced by the vernacular literature of the

later Celts themselves and by archaeological evidence. In an environment where the worlds of the living and the dead were closely intertwined, it is hardly surprising. The Otherworld was perceived as being very much like that of mortal men but without pain, disease or old age. In Irish myth it was called *Tir na n'Og* (the land of eternal youth) and was regarded as a place of peace and beauty. The Welsh called it *Annwn*. Pwyll, Lord of Dyfed, is said to have dwelt there for a year, saying that:

> 'Of all the courts he had seen on earth, it was the best-furnished with meat and drink, and vessels of gold and royal jewels.'

For all this, the Otherworld was an ambiguous place, full of shadows and hidden menace. The Celtic gods of death are always portrayed as dark, fearsome beings. And yet, seemingly, it was not a place where the dead would stay indefinitely. One of the main tenets of the philosophy of the Druids was the transmigration of the soul. Caesar wrote: 'The Druids attach particular importance to the belief that the soul does not perish but passes from one body to another after death.'

The cult of the severed head

The Celts believed that the dwelling place of the immortal soul was the head. To possess an enemy's head was to possess his soul. As with so many aspects of the warrior's life, the taking of an opponent's head in battle, and preferably as the result of single combat, had a mystical significance. But it was this gruesome practice that was regarded as the most barbaric characteristic of the Celtic warrior by the more 'civilised' Greeks and Romans, who were appalled at the desecration of the bodies of the dead on moral and religious grounds. Diodorus Siculus wrote:

> 'When their enemies fall, they cut off their heads and fasten them to the bridles of their horses; and handing over to their retainers the arms of their opponents all covered with blood, they carry them off as booty, singing a song of victory. These first fruits of victory they nail to the sides of their houses just as men do in certain kinds of hunting with the heads of wild beasts they have killed. They embalm the heads of their most distinguished foes in cedar oil and carefully preserve them. They show them to visitors, proudly stating that they had refused a large sum of money for them.'

In the light of Diodorus' account we may conclude that, apart from being tangible proof of the courage and prowess of the warrior, the head of the fallen enemy became an important prestige object. The care in its preservation, the pride in its exhibition and the fact that it was considered to be of great value not only to the warrior who had taken it but also to others, reveals a deeply felt bond between the victor and the vanquished.

The importance and extent of the cult of the severed head among the Celts is demonstrated by their display in shrines, either mounted in stonework as at La Roquepertuse in southern Gaul, or on wooden poles as at the hill-fort at Bredon Hill in western Britain. It is interesting to note that in both instances the heads were set up at the entrances. Perhaps the souls of these unfortunate warriors were now being used to

This iron spearhead with bronze decoration was recovered from the Thames and dates to the late Iron Age. Probably not used in battle but, like the Battersea Shield and Waterloo Helmet, made for display and as an offering to the gods. (Copyright: The British Museum)

provide symbolic protection for their enemies' strongholds? In Welsh and Irish myth, the severed head is imbued with supernatural power. When Bendigeitfran, one of the principal heroes in the cycle of Welsh legends called the *Mabinogion*, is mortally wounded in battle, he commands his own men to cut off his head and bury it in London facing east to guard Britain against foreign invasion.

The spoils of war

To the victor went the spoils of war. In addition to the heads of the vanquished, cattle, gold and women were especially prized as booty. Acquisition of wealth, and thereby status and prestige, was one of the principal motives that drove the Celtic warrior to wage war. The rich pickings to be had in the Mediterranean lands drew groups of mercenaries, and even entire tribes, like moths to a flame. Polybius describes how, on the eve of the battle of Telamon, they had become victims of their own success:

> 'The commanders of the Gauls . . . held a council of war. At this, Aneroestes argued that since they had now captured so much booty (for the number of prisoners and cattle, and the quantities of plunder they had taken were enormous) they should not give battle again and put all their gains at risk, but should return home in safety.'

Wise words on the part of Aneroestes. However, the amount of loot they had amassed slowed the Celtic army so much that it was caught by the Romans and destroyed. As for Aneroestes himself, his fate is outlined below (see page 55). Booty taken in war was not intended for the warrior's personal use, the exception being the head of an opponent killed in single combat. It was merely the means to an end. Just as pledges were made and oaths given between warriors at the feast, so were similar vows made to the gods before setting off on campaign. Caesar tells us that:

> ' . . . they vow to Mars the booty that they hope to take and after a victory they sacrifice the captives, both animal and human, and collect the rest of the spoils in one spot. Among many of the tribes great piles can be seen on consecrated ground. It is almost unknown for anyone, in defiance of religious law, to conceal his booty at home or to remove anything placed there. Such a crime is punishable by a terrible death under torture.'

Consecrated ground usually implied a sacred grove of oak trees (the *drunemeton*). The remains of man-made sanctuaries have also been discovered in Britain, Gaul and Italy. A more widespread practice, and one that was not limited to the Celts, was the ritual deposit of all manner of objects to the gods in natural springs, lakes and rivers. Water was a powerful manifestation of the supernatural, perhaps through its intimate connection with the earth and as a way of reaching the Otherworld. The dying Arthur was taken across the lake to be made whole again in Avalon, while his sword, Excalibur, was cast into the water. The site at La Tène is also believed to be a place where objects were ritually offered to the gods. In Britain, several rich finds have been recovered from the river Thames and in particular from Llyn Cerig Bach on the Druids' holy island of Anglesey. An idea of the scale of Celtic ritual deposits in watercourses can be gained by the supposed 50 tonnes of gold looted by the Romans at Tolosa (Toulouse) in 107 BC. Whether or not this figure can be credited, Caesar was apparently able to clear his debts and finance his future career with his share of the spoils from the war in Gaul.

Sacrifice

Several classical authors confirm that offerings to the gods included warriors taken in battle. Caesar wrote:

> ' . . . [the Gauls] who are engaged in the perils of battle either sacrifice human victims or vow to do so, employing Druids as ministers . . . For they believe that unless a man's life is paid for another's, the majesty of the gods may not be appeased.'

The Galatae of Asia Minor were held in dread because of their reputation for sacrificing prisoners of war, and enemies would prefer to commit suicide rather than fall into their hands. Human sacrifice held a particularly horrid fascination for the Greeks and Romans, yet how else are we to interpret the execution of Vercingetorix after being paraded through the streets of Rome?

Caesar's comment (see above) emphasises the ritual nature of the sacrifice. It was no mere crude butchery; it had its allotted place in the belief system of the Celts and served a specific purpose for the warrior. The sacrifice represented the gift of something of value. The greater the value of the gift the more powerful was the act of propitiation. In offering a captive for sacrifice the warrior fulfilled his vow made to the gods in the presence of the Druids, and at the same time he enhanced his status both in this world and in the Otherworld.

The sacrifice of prisoners was a method of divination. Strabo describes how the individual to be sacrificed would be stabbed in the back and his death throes studied closely to interpret the will of the gods. Others would have their throats cut over a sacred cauldron. There is also strong circumstantial evidence that, on occasion, a willing victim was killed to act as a messenger to the Otherworld. The remarkably well preserved remains of a young man, dubbed Lindow Man after the site in Cheshire, England, where he was discovered, have been considered in this light. His state of health, the care taken with his appearance (he had manicured nails), the traces of mistletoe found in his stomach (indicative of participation by the Druids) and the threefold manner of his death (a blow to the head, strangulation and the cutting of his throat), followed by the deposition of the body in water, all hint very strongly that this was no ordinary sacrifice. Although there are very few allusions to human sacrifice in Celtic vernacular literature, an Irish tradition provides a parallel for Lindow Man. A king was ritually killed by burning, wounding and drowning at Samhain, the modern Hallowe'en, the time of the year when the barrier between the world of men and the Otherworld vanished almost entirely.

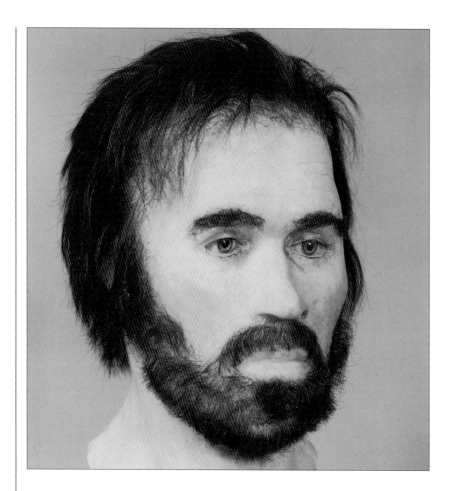

A remarkable reconstruction of the head of the sacrificial victim whose preserved remains were discovered in a peat bog in Cheshire. The circumstances surrounding this man's death seem to indicate that his was no ordinary sacrifice and that he may have gone willingly as a messenger to the Otherworld. (Copyright: The British Museum)

Slavery

Slavery was not widespread in Celtic society; it did not fit in well with the social structure in which patron and client supported each other to their mutual benefit. However, after increased contact with the Mediterranean, slaves became more valuable as a trading commodity. It was a trend that would contribute to the growing intensity of warfare between the Celts themselves. The fate of the great majority of warriors taken in battle, therefore, was to be sold. They were simply too valuable to be sacrificed.

As we have already noted, Diodorus Siculus remarked that a Celtic slave could be bought in exchange for an amphora of wine. The seller would share the traded wine among his followers to enhance his status. As the demand grew for wine and other Mediterranean prestige goods so did the need to find more slaves to barter. Celt and Roman soon came to depend on one another. Thousands of slaves a year were required to maintain the labour force in Italy in the 1st century BC. Not all came from Britain and Gaul though Caesar's campaigns brought in vast numbers, on occasions whole populations. Some warriors found a kind of honourable death in the arena, but most ended their days in the fields toiling to produce the very wine they coveted so much.

Ritual suicide

54 Although a fight to the death rather than a humiliating surrender was to be preferred, there were times when this was not possible. Rather than be taken alive, therefore, and suffer torture and death, or be sold into slavery at the hands of his captors, the warrior would commit suicide in a final act of honour. Polybius tells us of Aneroestes, a Celtic noble at Telamon who:

> '. . . fled from the battlefield with a few of his followers, and found a refuge where he and the whole of his retinue took their own lives.'

Other examples are not lacking, including Brennus following the retreat of the Galatae from Delphi, and perhaps the best known of all, Boudicca after the collapse of the revolt of the Iceni. Caesar's reference to Catuvolcus of the Eburones, who committed suicide by hanging himself from an elm tree hints strongly at the ritual nature of this act, a self-sacrifice in fact. The striking image that stood in the temple of Athene in Pergamon and which showed a warrior stabbing himself having just killed his wife, is a clear indication of the impact of the Celtic warrior's moral code of conduct on the Greek and Roman mind.

Ever conscious of his personal standing and his obligations in this world, and his geissi sworn to the gods in the Otherworld, failure was simply not an option to the Celtic warrior. To fail on the field of battle– where he sought to fulfil the boasts and pledges he had made at the feast and thereby gain even greater prestige, and where his every action could be judged – was personally and socially unacceptable. Honour demanded that the highest price be paid.

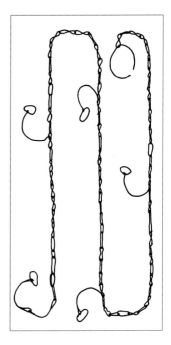

Following an increase in contact with the Mediterranean world, slaves became a valuable Celtic export commodity. They were traded for Greek and Roman prestige goods, especially wine.

The grave and beyond

Even in death the Celtic warrior could proclaim his status. The burial of a warrior together with his weapons, jewellery and other personal possessions not only reflected his belief in an afterlife and the immortality of the soul but also said a great deal about his rank. Many of the greatest surviving Celtic treasures have been discovered in graves. Cemeteries in East Yorkshire, England, and the Marne region in France have provided some of the best examples of warrior graves. However, burial was only one of the ways in which the Celts disposed of their dead. Caesar wrote of the Gauls:

> 'Their funerals are magnificent and expensive. They cast into the fire everything, even living creatures, which they believe to have been dear to the departed in life.'

In Iberia, the Vaccaei fed the bodies of those who had lived and died in war to vultures, believing the bird to be sacred – an obvious parallel with the crow and raven.

Caesar's reference to cremation was an indication of a growing practice among the Gauls in the 1st century BC, possibly influenced by Mediterranean custom. But throughout the Celtic world the vast majority of the dead, warriors or not, are undetectable from an archaeological point of view. It is thought that many were buried temporarily or exposed to the elements until the flesh had rotted from the corpse, a process called 'excarnation', after which the bones were

This assembly of grave goods, including wine jars and other items intended for the feast, emphasises the standing of the deceased British noble. (Copyright: The British Museum)

removed, in whole or in part, to be used in further rituals. This may explain the large number of dismembered skeletons carefully placed in the ritual pits and enclosures of the larger sanctuaries in northern Gaul.

The fame and renown gained by the warrior in life would live on after his death. The heroism and valour of the dead were extolled in song by bards at the feast as an example to the living. Some tales grew in the telling until they became part of Celtic myth and legend. Others remained part of history. In the 6th century AD, the British poet Aneirin wrote a fitting epitaph for the Celtic warriors who rode out to meet the Saxons at the battle of Catraeth:

'Three hundred gold-torqued warriors attacked, defending their land; there was slaughter. Though they were killed, they slew, and until the end of the world they will be remembered.'

Chariot or vehicle burials provide an indication of the status of the deceased. Some of the finest have been discovered at sites in East Yorkshire such as here, from Garton. Note the items of metalwork placed with the body. (Copyright: The British Museum)

GLOSSARY

Annwn: The Otherworld in Welsh myth and legend.

Bards: Poets who praised or satirised the warrior in song and who recounted the exploits of the heroes of Celtic legend.

Cantref: Welsh term for a group or retinue of warriors.

Carnyx: Long-necked war horn with a mouth often in the form of an animal.

Celts (Greek 'Keltoi', Latin 'Celtae'): Generic name given to the inhabitants of central and western Europe north of the Alps in the late pre-Roman Iron Age (c. 500 BC to c. AD 100). Their origins and how to define them are still a matter of much controversy. Most commonly defined as those peoples speaking dialects of the Indo-European family of languages now known as Celtic and/or displaying many of the elements of La Tène culture.

Celtiberians: The inhabitants of central and northern Spain in the late pre-Roman Iron Age. Apart from their Celtic language there was little to distinguish them from the Iberian peoples in the south and east of the Peninsula.

Celtic Migrations: Term given to the large-scale movements of Celtic peoples from west-central Europe to northern Italy and along the Danube basin in the first half of the 4th century BC. Several tribes subsequently settled in Asia Minor. The causes of these migrations remain unclear though overpopulation is believed to be one of the main factors.

Clientage: An agreement of mutual obligation by which a lower ranking member of Celtic society (the client) would pledge allegiance to an individual of higher rank (the patron) in exchange for security, patronage and employment. A similar system often linked entire clans and tribes.

Cubit: An ancient unit of measurement corresponding to the length of the forearm. Approximately 45cm (18 inches).

Druids: Privileged class of priests, law givers and guardians of tribal tradition. Known with certainty only in Britain, where they were said to have originated, and in Gaul. The Galatae had tribal judges who probably fulfilled a similar role.

Drunemeton: Translates as 'oak sanctuary'. A grove of oak trees ('drus' - oak) held to be particularly sacred to the Celts.

Excarnation: The process whereby a corpse is exposed to the elements or temporarily buried until the flesh has rotted from the bones, which are then reburied and/or used in further ritual.

Fianna: Irish term for a group or retinue of warriors.

Gaesatae: 'Spear bearer' hence 'warrior' because in Celtic society a man who bore a spear belonged to that class whose role was to fight. Compare 'ash-bearer' in early Anglo-Saxon society (spears were often made of ash wood). A large group of Celtic mercenary warriors who crossed the Alps to join the Celtic tribes of northern Italy in their struggle against Rome in the late 3rd century BC. Characterised by their practice of fighting naked.

57

Gaesum: A large Celtic spear.

Galatae: Greek name given to the Celtic tribes who settled in Asia Minor after the defeat of the Celts in Greece in the first half of the 3rd century BC.

Gallia Cisalpina: 'Gaul on this (i.e. the Roman) side of the Alps'. Roman province established in the late 3rd century BC on the territory of the Celtic tribes in northern Italy.

Gallia Transalpina: 'Gaul on the far side of the Alps'. Roman province established in the late 2nd century BC on the territory of the Celtic tribes of southern France. Later known simply as *Provincia* (the Province), hence modern Provence.

Galli (Gauls): Roman name given to the Celtic peoples in northern Italy and France.

Geissi: Taboos or sacred rules of conduct imposed on or voluntarily accepted by the Celtic warrior.

Halstatt: Archaeological site in Austria discovered in the early 19th century. The finds from the site were identified as belonging to the early pre-Roman Iron Age (*c*. 8th to 5th centuries BC) to which it gave its name. The Halstatt period is now considered to extend back into the late Bronze Age (from *c*. 1200 BC), but it is mainly characterised by early Iron Age princedoms, centres of power in eastern France and southern Germany. With the introduction of iron-working technology from the 8th century BC onwards, many of the elements of Celtic culture began to appear.

La Tène: Archaeological site in Switzerland discovered in the mid-19th century. Believed to have been a religious sanctuary, the rich finds at La Tène were identified as similar to others from northern France and the Rhineland, areas which rose to prominence following the collapse of the Halstatt princedoms. The later pre-Roman Iron Age is now referred to as the La Tène period and the name is widely associated with the material culture of the Celts.

Men of Art: Irish term given to the class in Celtic society that included artisans, metal workers, bards and Druids.

Palm: An ancient unit of measurement corresponding to the width of the palm. Approximately 10 cm (4 inches).

Potlach: Ostentatious distribution or redistribution of prestige items such as gold or wine among a warrior's retinue or to others in general, often given in the context of the feast to enhance the giver's status.

Tir na n'Og: The Otherworld in Irish myth and legend.

Torc: Neckring usually made of finely worked gold or other precious metals. Worn as a symbol of rank by high status warriors and probably of ritual significance.

Trimarcisia: Translates as 'group of three horsemen' and has its origins in the word *macha* (horse). Term used to describe a Celtic manner of fighting on horseback whereby the mounted warrior is supported by two retainers who provide him with a fresh horse, protect him if wounded and replace him in battle as required.

BIBLIOGRAPHY

Primary Sources

Caesar, *The Conquest of Gaul*
Diodorus Siculus, *Historical Library*
Livy, *History of Rome*
Pausanias, *Description of Greece*
Polybius, *The Histories*
Strabo, *Geography*
Tacitus, *The Agricola*

Jackson, KH (tr), *A Celtic Miscellany*
Kinsella, T (tr), *Táin bo Cuailnge*
Gantz, J (tr), *Early Irish Myths and Sagas*
Gantz, J (tr), *Mabinogion*

Secondary Sources

Beresford-Ellis, P, *The Celts in Italy*, St. Martins Press (London, 1998)

Collins, John, *The European Iron Age*, Batsford (London, 1992)
Cunliffe, Barry, *Iron Age Britain*, Batsford (London, 1993)
Cunliffe, Barry, *The Ancient Celts*, Oxford University Press (Oxford, 1997)
Cunliffe, Barry, *Greeks, Romans and Barbarians*, Batsford (London, 1988)
Cunliffe, Barry, *Wessex to AD 1000*, Longman (London, 1993)
Cunliffe, Barry, *Danebury*, Batsford (London, 1993)
Cunliffe, Barry (Ed), *The Oxford Illustrated Prehistory of Europe*, Oxford University Press
    (Oxford, 1994)
Evans, Stephen, *Lords of Battle*, Boydell Press (London, 1997)
Green, Miranda, *Celtic Myths*, British Museum Press (London, 1993)
Green, Miranda, *The Sun Gods of Ancient Europe*, Batsford (London, 1991)
Green, Miranda (Ed), *The Celtic World*, Routledge (London, 1995)
Guyonvarc'h, C-J & Le Roux, F, *La Civilisation celtique*, Payot (Paris, 1995)
Hunter, J & Rawlston, I (Eds), *The Archaeology of Britain*, Routledge (London, 1999)
Hutton, Ronald, *The Pagan Religions of the Ancient British Isles*, BCA (London, 1991)
James, Simon, *Exploring the World of the Celts*, (London, 1993)
James, Simon, *The Atlantic Celts*, British Museum Press (London, 1999)
Powel, TGE, *The Celts*, Thames and Hudson (London, 1980)
Ritchie, WF & JNG, *Celtic Warriors*, Shire (1985)
Ross, Ann, *Druids*, Tempus (London, 1999)
Solway, Peter, *Roman Britain*, Oxford University Press (Oxford 1981)
Stead, IM, *Celtic Art*, British Museum Press (London, 1993)
Wilcox, Peter, *Rome's Enemies (2): Gallic and British Celts*, Osprey (London, 1985)

PLACES TO VISIT

Museums:

The British Museum, London
The National Museum of Scotland, Edinburgh
The National Museum of Wales, Cardiff
The National Museum of Ireland, Dublin
The Museum of the Iron Age, Andover, Hampshire
Musée des Antiquites Nationales, St Germain-en-Laye, France
Musée de la Civilisation Gallo-Romaine, Lyon, France
Musée Calvet, Avignon, France
Musée Historique, Marseille, France
Musée Royaux d'Art et d'Histoire, Brussels, Belgium
Museo Numantino, Soria, Spain

Sites of interest:

Maiden Castle, Dorset, England
Danebury Hill-fort, Hampshire, England
Castell Henllys, Pembrokeshire, Wales
Tara, County Meath, Republic of Ireland
Glanum Gallo-Roman Town, St. Rémy de Provence, France
Entremont Hill-fort Settlement, Aix-en-Provence, France
Numantia Celtiberian City, Soria, Spain

Reconstructions:

Butser Ancient Farm, Petersfield, Hampshire, England
Parc Archéologique de Samara, Amiens, France
L'Archéodrome, Beaune, France

THE PLATES

A: GALLIC NOBLE WARRIOR, 1ST CENTURY BC

This man represents a Celtic noble at the time of Caesar's campaigns in Gaul. As a high-ranking warrior he displays his status by his appearance and by the quality of his dress and equipment. He is clean-shaven apart from his long moustache, which proclaims his nobility. As a further sign of his high status he wears a gold torc (**1**), which in this case is based on the hoard discovered at Ipswich. His tunic is of rare and costly silk, and his cloak is of fine wool fastened by a bronze brooch at the right shoulder (**2**).He wears a sunwheel medallion (**3**). Over the tunic he wears a shirt of iron ring mail. His iron helmet is based on the Agen model found at Alesia. Its functional design reflects the changing face of battle and the grim reality of total war against Rome. He is armed with a thrusting spear, the symbol of the free warrior. Its ash shaft is tipped with a bronze butt spike. As a noble, he also carries a sword (**4**). The example here is based on finds from the Thames.

Celtic shields (**5**) were generally oval or an elongated hexagon in shape, made of thin planks of oak or lime wood and covered with leather. The resulting construction was both light and resilient, essential to the warrior who held it by a central horizontal handgrip (**6**), wielding the shield not only to defend himself but also as an offensive weapon to punch at his opponent. His hand was protected by a hollow wooden boss that sometimes extended into a central spine to reinforce the face of the shield, which was itself reinforced by a bronze or iron boss plate. More rarely, the shield might have been edged with a metal strip. Examples discovered at La Tène measure approximately 1.1 x 0.6m (3ft 7ins x 2ft). However, later depictions from Gaul in the 1st century BC suggest an increase in size to 1.3 or even 1.4 metres (4ft 3ins or 4ft 7ins) in length, perhaps under the influence of the large body shields used by the Romans.

Diodorus Siculus wrote that Celtic shields were decorated 'in individual fashion', though there is little archaeological evidence as to what form this might have taken. The Roman monumental arch at Orange in southern France provides some details. However, its accuracy remains uncertain as the arch itself dates from the 1st century AD. A further and possibly firmer indication is given by the stylised figure of a boar that originally appeared on the Witham shield. It is likely that the warrior embellished his shield with such stylised representations of his personal totem or guardian spirit, or perhaps a more general Otherworld symbol such as the sunwheel to invoke their protective power. The example shown here is the horse.

B: THE BATTLE OF TELAMON, 225 BC

The Roman victory at the battle of Telamon in 225 BC broke the power of the Celts in northern Italy. Large numbers of Celtic warriors, known as Gaesatae (spear bearers) came south over the Alps at the invitation of the Boii and the Insubres in search of glory and plunder. For the raid across Etruria, 50,000 foot and 20,000 horse and chariots are said to have assembled but they were later obliged to withdraw, laden down with loot, in the face of the advancing Romans. At Telamon the Celts were caught between two converging Roman forces and were utterly destroyed.

The Gaesatae formed a distinct grouping outside the normal structure of Celtic society and could be compared with the Jomsvikings and Native American warrior societies. The principal characteristic that made them immediately identifiable on the battlefield was their custom of fighting naked. Their ritual nudity was probably linked to the sacred rules of conduct that governed many aspects of the warrior's life. It engendered a strong *esprit de corps* among the members of such groups and, according to Polybius, 'a proud confidence in themselves'.

However, Polybius' account of them at Telamon reveals that such confidence was not always well placed:

'When the light troops advanced in front of the legions and began to hurl their weapons, the naked warriors in the front ranks found themselves in a difficult situation. The shield used by the Gauls does not cover the whole body, and the stature of these naked warriors made the javelins all the more likely to find their mark. After a while, unable to drive off the light troops who were out of reach and who continued to rain volleys on them, their nerve broke under the ordeal. Some rushed forward in a blind fury, throwing away their lives as they tried to close with the enemy; others gave ground and fell back creating disorder among their comrades. In this way, the martial ardour of the Gaesatae was broken.'

The Gaesatae depicted here are suffering under a hail of Roman javelins. Two of them have lime-washed hair, a sign that they have adopted the horse as their personal totem and have entrusted themselves to the protection of the otherworldly power of the sun god. The figure on the right wears the long moustache and gold torc that proclaim his noble status. He is about to launch himself in rage and frustration at the Roman light troops who stay out of range.

C: ARMS AND EQUIPMENT – THE BLACKSMITH'S ART

Smiths formed part of the privileged class in Celtic society and were regarded as 'men of art'. Their specialist skills were highly valued by the warriors who patronised them for the arms, equipment and fine metalwork.

(**1**) Spearheads from La Tène. Many different types of spearheads have been found, their size, shape and weight indicating a variety of uses. Ash was a common wood for the shaft, which was fitted with a bronze butt spike (**2**) to provide a counterweight for the head. In Irish tales, spearshafts are described as having 'bands from head to foot', perhaps also of bronze. Two complete spears were recovered from the lake deposits at La Tène, each 2.5m (8ft) long.

(**3**) Swords. Until about 250 BC blades tended to be shorter: examples found at La Tène measure 0.66m (2ft) in length. With improvements in iron-working skills and the evolution of fighting styles, particularly in response to the increasing role of the mounted warrior, longer blades became more common in the last two centuries BC: on average 0.7 to 0.8m (2ft 4ins to 2ft 8ins). Swords were worn on the right, suspended from a bronze or iron chain (**4**) around the waist. The chain passed through a loop at the back of the scabbard and kept the weapon upright, helping to prevent the sword from becoming entangled with the warrior's legs as he walked or ran.

Dionysius of Halicarnassus described how the warrior would raise his sword above his head to deliver a downward stroke with his whole weight behind it. Together with the weight of the weapon itself, such a blow was capable of cutting through shield, armour and bone. When the legendary Cúchulainn faced the champion Edarcomhol: '. . . he struck him on the top of his head and split him to the navel.'

The reconstruction of the Kirkburn sword and scabbard shows the remarkable skill and craftsmanship of the Celtic blacksmith. The original was made from over 70 pieces of iron, bronze and copper, and was inlaid with enamel and glass.

(5) Helmets. Iron gradually replaced bronze once iron-working skills had been perfected. This change may also have been a consequence of the development of the long slashing sword and the role of cavalry. The grim reality of war against Rome is illustrated by the functional design of helmets from the 1st century BC.

(6) Mail. The manufacture of chain or ring mail was a lengthy process, requiring the highest standard of metal-working. Surviving fragments reveal two different methods: alternating rows of punched out rings with loops butted together, and rings that were riveted.

(7) Shields. Together with the spear, shields formed the basic panoply of the warrior. Their construction could also be complex, especially ceremonial models, such as the bronze Chertsey shield shown here, which was designed as a gift to the gods rather than for use in war.

D: FOSTERING AND CLIENTAGE, SOUTHERN BRITAIN EARLY 1ST CENTURY AD

'They do not allow their sons to approach them in public until they are old enough to bear arms, and they regard it as unbecoming for a son who is still a boy to stand in his father's sight in a public place.'

This comment by Caesar of the Gauls is probably a reference to the Celtic practice of fostering children in the household of a relative or patron. In the Táin, the female Pictish chieftain Aife says of the son she has just borne Cúchulainn:

'This day seven years I will send him to Ireland.'

The boy would spend the next seven years with others like him who would become his foster brothers, a relationship that was often far stronger than ties of blood and which reinforced the ethos of the warrior and the fianna. At the age of 14 he would attain manhood and gain the right to bear arms.

Fostering was an extension of clientage, the system of mutual obligation whereby an individual of lower rank (the client) pledged allegiance to one of higher rank (the patron) in exchange for security, patronage and, in the case of 'men of art' (bards, artisans, smiths, etc), employment. Both patron and client pledged their personal honour and risked disgrace, ruin and even death should they break their word. Clientage was a major element in the structure of Celtic society.

Here we see a young boy obliged to hide from his father, who has caught him by surprise on a visit to his patron into whose household the boy has been fostered. Though each is aware of the other's presence, neither will acknowledge the fact and the boy will remain out of sight. Honour is therefore preserved.

The noble chieftain is accompanied by two members of his retinue who act as bodyguards. The client warrior is accomapanied by his shieldbearer, his closest companion. Bodyguards and shieldbearer are armed with light spears. Except for a dagger, both patron and client are unarmed as a gesture of confidence and friendship. The chieftain's farmstead is based on the reconstructed Great Roundhouse and other buildings at Butser Ancient Farm in Hampshire, England.

E: CELTIC MOUNTED WARRIOR, ITALY 3RD CENTURY BC

'. . . some Gallic horsemen came in sight carrying heads hanging from their horses' breasts and fixed on their spears, singing their usual song of triumph.'

According to Livy, this was the first indication that the Romans had of a defeat at the hands of the Senones, a Celtic tribe from Cisalpine Gaul in 295 BC. The warrior shown here is one of the victorious Gallic horsemen. He wears a helmet with a horsehair crest befitting a mounted warrior, gold bracelets (1) and a newly developed mail-shirt with decorated fastening (2). His horse's harness is richly decorated with bronze plaques representing human heads.

Although their main strength lay in their infantry, the Celts were accomplished horsemen. Caesar tells us that the Gauls were prepared to pay large sums for good horses. Depictions of Celtic horsemen on finds from Halstatt indicate that the horse was ridden in war as well as harnessed to a chariot from the early Iron Age. Both were the preserve of the noble warrior, who viewed battle as a way to enhance his status by single combat. Pausanias wrote that Celtic warriors rode onto the battlefield and then dismounted to engage the enemy. It seems fairly certain, therefore, that the Trimarcisia (whereby the noble was accompanied and supported by two retainers) did not constitute a tactical fighting unit in the sense that the Greeks or Romans understood the term.

Celtic mercenary horsemen, especially the Gauls and the Celtiberians, were highly regarded, fighting for Carthage in the Second Punic War and later on behalf of Rome when they provided Caesar with much of his mounted arm. The growing emphasis on cavalry among the Celts from the end of the 3rd century BC can be seen in the increasing length of sword blades, some almost 90cms (35ins) in length, too long to be easily wielded by a warrior on foot. The change in emphasis can perhaps be explained by the introduction of the four-pommel saddle (3). This type of saddle, which is thought to have originated among the nomadic tribes of the Asiatic steppe from where it spread to central and western Europe in the latter half of the 1st millennium BC, provided the rider with a seat that was as secure as if he were using stirrups, which had not yet been invented, although spurs were used (4). In addition, there is convincing archaeological evidence of improvements in the breeding of horses in the last two centuries BC, especially in parts of Gaul. Significantly, there is little evidence of this practice in Britain. (5) shows a reconstruction of a snaffle bit.

F: SINGLE COMBAT, ITALY 3RD CENTURY BC

Single combat was one of the most effective ways for the warrior to gain or enhance his prestige. In offering a challenge publicly on the battlefield he fulfilled the boasts made at the feast, confirming his honour and at the same time calling into question that of his opponent. It was an integral part of the Celtic way of war that enabled the greatest and most ambitious warriors to play their own individual part in the ritual of battle. Their courage would be remembered in the songs of the bards together with the heroes of Celtic myth and legend. Single combat also served to increase tension among the other warriors who were working themselves into a frenzy with war cries and the clashing of weapons on shields.

In other discussions on Celtic warfare and society, it has been suggested that the ritual of single combat was a way of limiting conflicts which, while being an integral part of the social structure, was hedged around with conventions and taboos. Through single combat, the whole clan or tribe could participate in battle. Following a series of combats, the issue would be clearly decided and accepted by the onlookers who would then disperse. The role of the warrior was indeed governed by strict rules, but to assume that the fianna of the warrior who had just been killed and beheaded by his rival would meekly retire from the field, any more than the followers of the victor would stand by and watch them go when both were at a peak of frenzy, is to disregard many accounts of the Celts in battle and also the psyche of the warrior himself.

Here we see the outcome of one such combat. The young warrior portrayed is seeking to make a name for himself. He has challenged a Roman to single combat and displays his defeated enemy's head to the Celtic host who are about to launch themselves into battle. Single combat was also a recognised part of war in the Republican period among high-ranking Roman officers, many of whom were able to hold their own against their Celtic adversaries.

G: THE BATTLE OF THE SAMBRE, 57 BC

The wild charge of the Celtic warrior was the inevitable consequence of his battle frenzy, brought on by the sound of battle cries, war horns and the clash of weapons, and the sight of heroes engaging in single combat. It was rightly feared throughout the classical Mediterranean world. However, if those facing the charge were sufficiently prepared, protected and above all disciplined, then there was a good chance that the force of the attack could be blunted. Once this happened, the Celts' psychology of war worked against them. Celtic armies were, by their very nature, fragile and unstable, made up of masses of individual warriors all competing with one another for status and glory. If their initial charge failed to break the enemy line, the Celts would tend to become discouraged. Their battle frenzy would begin to ebb, the initiative would pass to the defenders, and they would almost certainly lose the battle. Despite the well-attested occasions when Celtic hosts fought stubbornly to the death, their lack of staying power in the face of more disciplined armies gave rise to their reputation for fickleness among the Romans, whose concept of battle was substantially different. Both parties considered that the other did not 'fight by the rules'.

The scene portrayed here shows the successful charge of the Nervii against Caesar's disorganised legions at the battle of the Sambre in northern Gaul in 57 BC. The Nervii had a particular reputation for ferocity among the Gallic tribes, whose forces were said to consist entirely of infantry. After observing the Roman army on the march and making optimum use of the close nature of their home terrain, which was mostly marsh and forest, the Nervii and their allies ambushed the unprepared legions while they were in the process of setting up camp. Brushing aside the Roman cavalry screen, the speed of the attack enabled the Nervii to reach and engage their opponents before they could react and form a coherent line of battle. Nevertheless, the morale of the Romans held, largely due to their training in formal units. The Gauls' limited use of armour and their more open formation required by their habit of individual combat, as well as the use by some of the long slashing sword made them vulnerable to the tactics of the Romans, whose shorter swords enabled them to fight in close order, protected by their helmets, mail-shirts and large shields.

H: BRITISH CHARIOT WARRIOR, EARLY 1ST CENTURY AD

'For journeys and in battle they use two-horse chariots, carrying both charioteer and chieftain.' (Diodorus Siculus)

Archaeological evidence suggests that the Celtic chariot was a specialised version of the two- and four-wheeled vehicles used in funerary rites in the early Iron Age. The chariot was a parade vehicle that emphasised the high status of the warrior who rode in it, but which was also intended for use in battle both as a means of transport and as a fighting platform. Caesar describes at some length the tactics employed by the Britons, who were the last Celtic people to use the chariot in war. The Celts in Gaul and elsewhere abandoned the chariot almost completely from the end of the 3rd century BC onwards, in favour of the individual warrior on horseback as fighting styles and technology evolved.

The chariot was simply a platform about 1m^2 (3ft 4in^2) carried on an axle (**1**) and a pair of spoked, iron-rimmed wheels approximately 0.9m (3ft) in diameter, and harnessed via a pole and a yoke to two ponies. The sides of the vehicle were double loops of bent wood. From depictions on coins it seems likely that at least parts of the sides were filled and decorated with wicker or leather panels. The front and rear of the chariot was left open for ease of access. The floor was possibly also of leather, providing a simple form of suspension.

To the Celts, both the wheel and the horse were symbols of the sun god; only the highest status warriors would have sufficient prestige to ride and fight in a chariot. The elite symbolic nature of the vehicle was reflected in the quality of the fittings and the care taken in its construction. Metalwork was often inlaid with enamel, glass and coral; a surviving wheel from Scotland was found to be made with three different woods. Harnesses were also richly decorated - see the decorated terrets and snaffle bit (**2**).

The scene depicted here shows a charioteer turning the chariot to the right, following the path of the sun from east to west, thus invoking its Otherworldly power but, at the same time, presenting the warrior's shielded side to his enemy, a move considered to be overtly hostile. Although not of the same social class as the noble warrior, the charioteer was his closest companion. Whether fighting from the vehicle or away from it, the noble's life was dependent on the charioteer's skill. The Táin has an interesting reference to the special status of the charioteer: ' . . . he placed the charioteer's sign on his brow . . . a circle of deep yellow shaped on an anvil's edge.'

I: AMBUSH AND SKIRMISH, SOUTHERN BRITAIN MID 1ST CENTURY BC

'When the Romans were busy foraging, scattered and with their weapons laid aside, the Britons suddenly attacked; they swarmed around with cavalry and chariots, killing a few and throwing the rest into confusion before they could form up.'

'There was a fierce engagement as the British cavalry and chariots clashed with our cavalry on the march. However, our men prevailed and drove the enemy into the woods and hills, killing a good many of them, though suffering a number of casualties themselves through pressing the pursuit too far. Then, after a while, when our men were off their guard and busy fortifying the camp, the Britons suddenly rushed out of the woods, charged down on the outposts on picket duty and started a fierce battle there.'

These two passages from Caesar provide a good illustration of the combined tactics used by Celtic horsemen and chariot warriors to harass and snipe at the Roman forces feeling their way in unfamiliar territory. Native British horses were smaller than those in Gaul, where cross-breeding had improved the stock. Caesar's longer description of battle against the Britons and their use of cavalry and chariots together in a mutually supporting role, suggests that the latter were still regarded as more becoming to the status of the noble warrior. The ambush and the sudden charge from cover were favoured tactics of the Celts, not only in Britain but throughout Europe, and recall the ritual of the raid with its emphasis on surprise attack, skirmish and the duel between high status warriors.

The scene pictured here portrays an attack by Cassivelaunus' forces on a Roman foraging party. Previous surprise attacks by the Britons have taught the Romans to keep some of their men under arms to form a rallying point. However, despite his best efforts Caesar's lack of sufficient cavalry on both his expeditions to Britain meant that he could do little to counter the constant threat posed to his foragers and lines of communication by the skirmishing, hit- and-run tactics of the Celts.

J: THE SPOILS OF WAR, GAUL EARLY 1ST CENTURY BC

Death was an inseparable part of the life of the Celtic warrior. He had no fear of it and on occasions welcomed it, seeking it out on the battlefield. A hero's death in war would ensure that his name and reputation would be remembered at the feast. Even if his death were self-inflicted through ritual suicide, his honour and standing would be maintained and even enhanced. However, for those warriors who suffered the humiliation of being taken alive in battle, a different fate could be expected, as part of the victor's spoils of war.

Enemies taken prisoner by the Celts in battle were dedicated to the gods. Booty consisted not only of gold and other precious objects together with arms and armour, but also captives, both human and animal. It was deposited on consecrated ground, often a grove of sacred oak trees, but on occasions a man-made sanctuary such as those discovered in northern France and elsewhere. To conceal or remove anything from these 'sacred precincts of the gods', as Diodorus Siculus termed them, was considered sacrilege and was punishable by death. Some prisoners were sacrificed to fulfil the vows taken by the warrior before the battle: 'a life given for a life spared'. The Druids, who formed the link between the world of men and the Otherworld in Celtic society, conducted all sacrifices.

The great majority of prisoners were not put to death but were sold to the slave traders who supplied the markets in Rome and the Mediterranean. As the demand for luxury prestige items, especially wine, increased among the Celtic nobility, captives were viewed as an easily obtainable trading commodity. A commodity, moreover, that was in constant demand. The interdependence between Celts and Romans grew from the time of the creation of the Roman province of Gallia Transalpina. It was a relationship that caused warfare to intensify among the Celts themselves, with slave-raiding as its principal objective.

The scene depicted here shows a group of warriors who have been taken in battle being sold to Roman middlemen in exchange for wine – one amphora per slave. Similar transactions would have taken place throughout central Gaul and probably in southern Britain too. Cicero remarked that Gaul was filled with Roman traders. The slaves would have been sent on to a trade emporium such as Châlons-sur-Saône and then south to the Roman Province and beyond. The slave chain is based on a find from Bigbury hill-fort in Kent.

INDEX

References to illustrations are shown in **bold**. Plates are shown with page and caption locators in brackets.